Continued on page 94

£1·70

CONTENTS

PHOTO STORIES

2 DANCE CRAZY!
8 SECRET LOVE
26 DREAM LOVER

42 HIGH NOON!
58 SHE'S MY GIRL
81 A WORLD WITHOUT LOVE

FASHION

14 PUZZLE IT OUT!
21 GOLDEN OLDIES!
66 SHOWSTOPPERS!

READERS' TRUE EXPERIENCES

40 I WAS A FOOL

50 A GIRL'S BEST FRIEND . . .
92 I WAS SCARED OF HIS SISTER

POP

11 GOOD LOOKERS!
49 EAT TO THE BEAT!
52 WELL, WHADDA YOU KNOW?
61 SCARY MONSTERS AND SUPER LEAPS!
65 A WEEK IN THE LIFE OF . . . DEBBIE HARRY
64 BIGGER-THAN-USUAL POPWORD!
86 BAD MANNERS ARE CATCHING!

SHORT STORIES

22 A WALK IN THE PARK
38 CHAINED UP CHARLIE AND THE CATERPILLAR KID
82 PLAYING CUPID

FEATURES

5 FEELING CHILLY
6 HOW TO GET WISE TO THE GUYS!
24 FUNNY FARM (1)
25 BRIGHTEN UP YOUR BEDROOM
33 IT'S TIME TO PUT ON MAKE-UP
34 HOW TO BE A PARTY SMARTY!

36 1982 STARTS HERE!
37 PUT YOUR CARDS ON THE TABLE!
54 HELP! I NEED SOMEBODY
56 FRIENDS — WHO NEEDS 'EM?
60 HOW WOULD YOU LABEL YOURSELF?
72 DETECT A FELLA!
74 I WISH I'D SAID THAT!
86 SIDESPLITTERS
90 FUNNY FARM (2)

BEAUTY

17 SHADY LADIES!
28 OFF WITH IT!
76 SAVE ENERGY — EXERCISE WITH A FRIEND!
78 BE DEMURE IN THE DAYTIME . . . AND DAZZLE AT NIGHT

QUIZZES

10 HEY — HOT LIPS
44 ARE YOU KIDDING?
70 ARE YOU INTRO, EXTRO OR JUST IN BETWEENO?

Ed Quarters

Presenting — by popular demand! — the first-ever Patches Annual! Tan-ta-ra-ra (fanfare of trumpets!).

We've had a lot of fun putting it together and we hope *you* have a lot of fun reading it. And just to put you in the mood, here's a picture of me!

Lots of super photo stories for you to curl up with — that's if your guy/dog/cat isn't available!! And no, I'm afraid we didn't cross the Atlantic to photograph the story on page 42. Instead we found our very own J.R. — well, J.B. actually! — who let us take over his ranch, Frontier City, in Berkshire, to act out the Patches version of "High Noon!" We had a great time there — who needs the Wild West!

As well as photo stories, there're quizzes, pop and fun features, fashion and beauty — you name it, we've got it here for you! So drop us a line — at Patches, 20 Cathcart Street, Kentish Town, London NW5 3BN — and let us know what you think of our very first Annual! And remember, you don't have to wait a whole year for more super stories 'n' stuff — order us every Friday from your newsagent!

Love,

The Ed

Printed and Published in Great Britain by D. C. Thomson & Co., Ltd. , 185 Fleet Street, London EC4A 2HS. © D. C. Thomson & Co., Ltd., 1981.

ISBN 0-85116-202-9

Feeling Chilly

Are you fed up of sitting shivering every winter, clutching a cup of coffee for warmth? Do you get tired of people shouting, "Hey, Rudolph!" as your nose flashes past? Follow this amazing Patches guide to beating the winter blues and you'll never have to put a silencer on your teeth again!

Buy a nice, big husky and wear him to school. If it snows too much, you can make a sledge in woodwork, say "Mush!" and he'll tow you home.

Crawl in with the tortoise and hibernate!

Sew yourself into a teddy bear outfit and look for someone to pick you up and cuddle you.

Drape a couple of

guinea-pigs over your head as ear-warmers. But — take care that you're not wearing the husky that day!

Start eating straight away to give yourself layers and layers of lovely, warming FAT. Emigrate to Turkey early in the spring — they *love* fat girls there!

Falling in love warms you up nicely inside (and if you keep kissing him, it'll prevent your teeth from chattering!).

Cut a hole in the middle of your duvet and wear it like a poncho. If you've already got your layers of fat, though, you'd be better to give this one a miss — otherwise you'll never get on the bus!

Stay in by the fire with a pair of your dad's old socks on, clutching a mug of cocoa. You won't mind a *bit* that your best friend has

braved the cold disco to nab all the best fellas, will you?

Get Gran to knit you matching ear muffs, foot muffs, hand muffs and nose muff.

Persuade Daddy to buy you a fur coat. Well, you don't see rabbits sneezing and blowing their little noses, do you?

Install central heating in your jeans.

Run everywhere! Not only will you be *warm* — you'll be fit!

Buy yourself 10 hot-water-bottles, fill 'em up — then strap 'em on to appropriate parts of your anatomy.

Fall in love with a St Bernard and teach it to sit on you. Not only will you be *warm* — you'll be flat! But if you ever get lost in the snow, at least he'll be handy with the brandy!

Shut yourself in the airing-cupboard next to the immersion heater.

Pretend you're an Eskimo and take to wearing fourteen fur coats — all at once!

Emigrate — to Australia for preference. Well, our winter's *their* summer, remember?!

Eat lots of curries — real roasters, as hot as you can stand them. It's sort of like having your own, personal central heating system!

Buy yourself a set of thermal underwear. Oh help, you say, have you *seen* them?! Yeah, hardly alluring are they? The thing is, they're fairly cheap and they actually work! You can put your lovely, warm, thermal vest on, and have something exquisite on top and nobody'll know how boringly sensible you're being underneath!

Snuggle up to your favourite guy. Your combined body heat will keep you both cosy — it's a fact! A fact, too, that mountain-rescue teams recommend bodily contact as a way of reviving people who've been exposed to dire, winter temperatures. Tell your guy you're going to give him a swift demonstration of rescue techniques for use in emergencies. Or you could tell him you're cutting central heating bills by cuddling. Persuade him that it's all purely in the interests of ecology — we're sure he'll be only too happy to

co-operate with either of these worthy causes!

Create a crowd. Wear something weird, or even better, point up to the sky saying, "Is it a bird? Is it a plane? Is it . . .? No — it couldn't be . . . could it?" Just point and gasp so lots of people will gather round you, breathing and gasping and keeping the chill winds from you.

A smashing way to keep warm is to think how really cold you'd be if you were stranded at sea clinging to a

single beam of wood, wearing only your bikini — helpless and screaming against roaring seas and lashing gales. Or imagine being transferred suddenly to the South Pole in your undies — now that'd be *really* cold.

Eat sensibly. Oh yawn, that old thing! Eating sensibly does help to fight the cold, though. It helps to fight off chills and flu, too. A good breakfast's the thing. No more of this dashing out into the blizzard in your six-inch stilettos after grabbing a bit of unbuttered toast and a sip of weak tea. Nope — a boiled egg, a couple of slices of wholemeal toast, a glass of fresh orange juice and a hot drink — now you're *really* ready to face the ice and snow!

Get angry — *really* angry — at something. Think about some world injustice or bring back a snippy remark a shop assistant made to you. Let your blood pump through

you, let yourself see red, let your eyeballs roll. Well — the Hulk doesn't ever seem the least goose-pimply at all does he? Must be something warming in anger!

Wear woollies — there are lots of really nice, fashionable ones around just now in lovely styles and colours. Or, if you can't afford that, did you know that newsprint is actually very good for protecting you from the chills? So why not line the inside of your clothes with all your old copies of Patches? You may crinkle a bit when you walk and rustle when you sit, but you'll always have something on hand (and foot and elbow) to read if you get bored!

HOW TO GET WISE TO THE GUYS!

*Would you fall for a flirt, drool over a drip or
pass out when you saw a punk?
Finding a guy is easy, finding the
right guy is a bit trickier, but follow our easy
guide to the six basic types of boy
and you won't go far wrong.*

IF the first guy you encounter has short, sleeked-back hair, the hint of a moustache and eyebrows that meet in the middle — watch it! You've just met Nigel —

THE MUMMY'S BOY

He's probably shy, and he's *definitely* got a mum who wants to tuck him up in bed every night at nine o'clock with a nice soothing glass of warm milk and his teddy! He won't so much *talk* to you as stammer, and when he does actually manage to get two sentences together, they'll include the yawn-words, "school," "youth-hostels" and "chosen career." If you encourage Nigel *at all,* he'll give you a blow-by-blow account of the innermost workings of the silicon chip, and, because he hasn't much sense of humour, he won't appreciate it if you

make remarks about thinking you had 'em with vinegar! Still, he's quite *sweet,* in a serious sort of way, and if you can tolerate him, he *will* grow up eventually (probably into an Insurance Salesman)! But if you're not too keen, at the moment, on hot milk and fussy mothers — maybe you'd better look the other way — fast!

When you do, if what you see is . . . Wearing a gold medallion with his shirt open to the waist, showing acres of hairy chest and a suntan (even in December!) and eyes that smile quickly while they flicker over everyone — be careful! This guy's —

THE POSER

Usually answering to the name of Justin or Howard, he's convinced he's the world's gift to every female from six to sixty-six, and nobody's ever going to give him "no" for an answer! The moment you meet, he'll take you

by the arm and ask you where you've been all his life. When you try to *tell* him, he won't be listening. He'll've found his reflection in *something* (your shoes, the glass he's holding, your eyes — *anything*!), and he'll be practically blowing kisses at himself! He'll talk, non-stop, about his plans for *his* future and how he's going to be the greatest thing since Elvis or Einstein. He'll *assume*, just because he's got an arm round you, that you're his property from now on, and if you take yourself off to another part of the room he'll spend the rest of the evening looking at you soulfully with big brown eyes that remind you of a hurt Cocker spaniel! Don't be fooled! The only thing that's hurt about him is his pride, and he'll probably go and drown his sorrows with another bottle of after-shave — until the next unsuspecting female comes along!

When you *get* to another part of the room, there's a fair chance that you'll bump into Walter or someone very like him. Walter is type number three —

THE WEED

He's a tall, thin guy wearing National-Health specs that don't fit, with a slight stoop, spots and a nose that started off in the next county! If he comes up to you — you've got two options! Pretend you haven't seen him — or visit the loo, pronto! It's an emergency! He is *intense*! He's never had a girlfriend, doesn't know why, and would very much like you to tell him please. He's got an inferiority complex several miles long, is sure his spots are something dire (like plague — not acne!) can't, he'll moan, see a *thing* without his glasses, has already started saving up for a guide dog, and

is going to visit this fantastic plastic surgeon, who gives discounts, about his nose just as soon as he's got two million pounds! He's completely obsessed by illness, and if you sneeze (because the stuff he rubbed on his chest before he came out made your nose tickle), he'll start panicking in case you've got Nasosinusitis. (You haven't — believe us! Honest!) He's very kind-hearted and generous — when it comes to looking after *himself*. But if you're daft enough to let him walk you home and it just *happens* to be raining outside — get ready to call an ambulance! He'll go down with imaginary pneumonia at any second — and *that* kind of kiss of life you can do without, can't you?

So, you've looked around and there's not a lot attracting your attention, apart from . . . oh dear. It's Tony —

THE FLIRT!

A nicely-built guy with slim hips, neat hair, laughing eyes and *slightly* sticking-out ears.

Well, it's entirely up to you, but do you happen to've noticed how many *other* girls he's been laughing at — apart from you, that is? Mmm? If you haven't, start counting now! Not only is he a flirt, y'see — he's a *two-timing* flirt! He's got a girlfriend in tow, but he's managed to lose her somewhere (like the car park. He promised he'd be back in three seconds, two hours ago!) and he's making the most of his time to see what other talent he can captivate. If you let him chat you up, you'll hear all the things you've ever wanted to hear — how beautiful you are, what a fantastic figure you've got, how your laugh sounds like the tinkle

of tiny, silver bells, etc., etc. With no trouble at all, he'll get you to a stage where you're just standing there with your eyes shut, waiting for him to kiss you. Careful! You may still be like that when the disco closes — and the moment you *do* open your eyes again, you'll see an awful lot of other females in exactly the same position!

But him? — he'll be back in the car park, telling his girlfriend how he risked life and limb because this pussy-cat was stuck up a tree and the old lady who owned it absolutely *begged* him to rescue it!

You're about to give up and drift off home sadly when you suddenly spot . . . Good grief! — it's an —

ORDINARY BOY!

Somebody quite slim, wearing faded, blue jeans, a sweat-shirt, sneakers and holding an anorak, with quite large eyes, a normal nose that turns up just a *little,* the odd freckle, hair that keeps falling over his forehead, and a sensible chin he's currently scratching thoughtfully . . . Quick!

Grab him! Get into conversation *at once*! He could be called Mike or John or Andy or Tom or Dick or Harry, but the important thing is that he's nice, reliable, affectionate, ordinary and has a sense of humour! And even more important, he's been hanging around all night just waiting to find somebody like you! *But maybe he looks just a tiny bit too* ordinary — 'specially as you've just spotted . . .

THE PUNK

Bob — or Gob as he prefers to be known — always wears black, has his

thumbs stuck in his belt, a quite nice mouth that quirks up at the corners, and eyes that you can't see 'cos they're hidden by sunglasses.

OK. As long as you're heavily into Gen X and the Stranglers and what went wrong when they filmed "The Great Rock 'n' Roll Swindle" and "Breaking Glass" — you'll be fine! If you're *not,* you'd be better off going home, 'cos Gobby-baby definitely *is*! He doesn't like *anything* — and that includes the opposite sex! He's got a chip on his shoulder because he was chucked out of secondary school for spray-canning the headmaster. His mum doesn't understand him. His dad doesn't understand him. And *he* doesn't care (or so he says)! Actually, underneath all this is a shy little soul trying to get out. He'd secretly like to have a nice girlfriend, wear a suit and get a job in a bank, but he's not at all sure how to go about it. If you give him *any* advice — he'll look as if he's going to sink his safety-pins into your throat, and he'll growl at you a lot. But if you walk away, he'll suddenly start ambling after you — because you just *happen* to be the only person who's talked to him all night, and he desperately wants a friend! He once had this budgie, y'see, only its feathers fell out and . . . Ahh! In other words, if you can get *underneath* that hard exterior and find the *real* person — he's potentially quite a nice guy!

But if you can't, have almost reached the cloakroom, gloomily wondering whether the 124 bus'll be on time, then why not try your luck again with that nice, ordinary boy? So who cares if he *is* the boy-next-door? Everybody's got to live some place — haven't they?

A rainy night in the bus station isn't the best place for excitement—or is it?

HEY, COME BACK! BLAST, I'VE MISSED IT . . .

ME TOO. AND IT'S HALF AN HOUR BEFORE THE NEXT.

SECRET LOVE

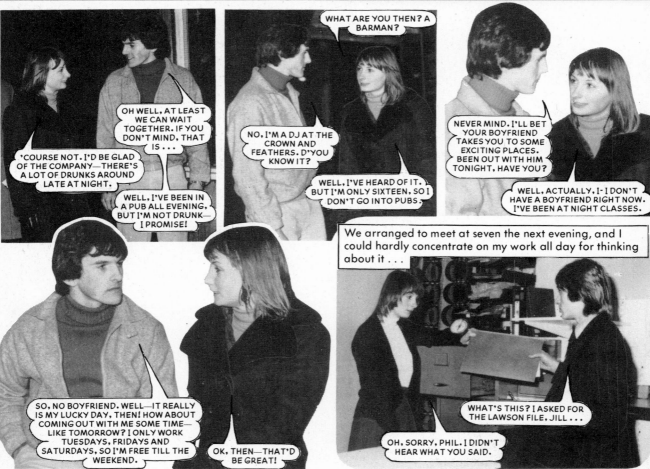

OH WELL, AT LEAST WE CAN WAIT TOGETHER. IF YOU DON'T MIND, THAT IS . . .

'COURSE NOT. I'D BE GLAD OF THE COMPANY—THERE'S A LOT OF DRUNKS AROUND LATE AT NIGHT.

WELL, I'VE BEEN IN A PUB ALL EVENING, BUT I'M NOT DRUNK—I PROMISE!

WHAT ARE YOU THEN? A BARMAN?

NO, I'M A DJ AT THE CROWN AND FEATHERS. D'YOU KNOW IT?

WELL, I'VE HEARD OF IT. BUT I'M ONLY SIXTEEN, SO I DON'T GO INTO PUBS.

NEVER MIND. I'LL BET YOUR BOYFRIEND TAKES YOU TO SOME EXCITING PLACES. BEEN OUT WITH HIM TONIGHT, HAVE YOU?

WELL, ACTUALLY, I-I DON'T HAVE A BOYFRIEND RIGHT NOW. I'VE BEEN AT NIGHT CLASSES.

SO, NO BOYFRIEND. WELL—IT REALLY IS MY LUCKY DAY, THEN! HOW ABOUT COMING OUT WITH ME SOME TIME—LIKE TOMORROW? I ONLY WORK TUESDAYS, FRIDAYS AND SATURDAYS, SO I'M FREE TILL THE WEEKEND.

OK, THEN—THAT'D BE GREAT!

We arranged to meet at seven the next evening, and I could hardly concentrate on my work all day for thinking about it . . .

WHAT'S THIS? I ASKED FOR THE LAWSON FILE, JILL . . .

OH, SORRY, PHIL. I DIDN'T HEAR WHAT YOU SAID.

8

Continued from page 9

12

HELEN DOOLEY told us how her hair always manages to look good.

"I like to have a slightly outrageous style for evenings and a normal one for daytime. So I like the technique where the underside of your hair is tinted or dyed red or purple or whatever. This means that during the day you can have a completely normal style, but in the evening you simply put your hair up and it reflects the real you!"

"I've always felt that nail varnishes should be chosen with great care," said RITA RAY. "There are so many that chip easily and then look dreadful, so it's well worth spending a bit of money on getting a really good one. Hard As Nails is quite reliable for strengthening, but you really just have to experiment until you find a brand that suits you."

Lips are important to BERNADETTE NOLAN.

"I take a lot of trouble with my lips," Bernadette said. "Some products smudge terribly. The correct way to apply any lipstick is to draw the outline first before filling in. You might find that a waterproof lipstick will suit you better. There's nothing worse than meeting a guy and not realising that your lipstick's spread over your face!"

THEREZE BAZAAR is someone who always looks good.

"Some girls go out and blow a lot of money on clothes and records," she told us, "but they overlook the most important thing, which is their face. They feel that clothes are a substitute for poor make-up. I'd rather save up and buy some expensive cosmetics, because if your face looks good, you can get away with a lot in the clothes area.

"One thing I've always done is put a good moisturiser on my face before applying any make-up. I choose Christian Dior, which might cost a bit more, but is well worth the feeling that my skin is lovely and soft."

GOOD-LOOKERS!

PATCHES pop

Discover the secrets of looking great – the stars' way!

"For me, making up is a form of relaxation," said TOYAH. "I spend at least an hour on my face trying out new products I've discovered and seeing what effects I can achieve. I carry all of my face gear in an old carpenter's toolbox wherever I go! I like to look dramatic, but I've discovered that when it comes to hair care, you've really got to be careful. I dyed my hair so much that it began to fall out, so I had to have it cut pretty short. Now it's growing again and I'll take more care of it. Excessive bleaching ruins your hair!"

"I've always bothered to take time to experiment with cosmetics," said SHEENA EASTON, "particularly eye-shadows which can do a lot for you. I think the really important thing is to get the balance right between daytime and night-time. What looks good under low lights in a club or at a disco can look dreadful when you're walking along a street.

"Biba's colours seem suited to me. I would never wear a green eye-shadow with a blue outfit or vice versa because they clash too much. Bronzes and beiges are much better because they go with most things."

HEY~ HOT LIPS

Would you rate smooching among your five fave pastimes or are lips just there to keep your teeth warm as far as you're concerned? Maybe kissing seems as natural as breathing to you or maybe you're about as passionate as the average potato! Why not have a go at our silly quiz and find out where *you* rate on the P.S.S. — the Patches Smooching Scale?

1. A very good-looking guy's been chatting you up and asking you to dance all evening at the disco. It's the last record — the Commodores' "Three Times A Lady" — and he comes up, leads you on to the floor, and wraps his arms around you for a smoochy dance. Before long, he's giving you a long, slow, loving kiss . . . What're you thinking?

a. Nothing at all. How can you possibly *think* at a time like this? Ah, bliss . . .

b. "Wonder if me mates, Sandra an' Betty'll wait for me in the cloakroom? Help!"

c. You're planning what deep, romantic remark you're going to make when the record stops and you gaze into each other's eyes.

2. When a guy's kissing you goodnight outside your house, you would usually . . .

a. have your hands in your pockets, and your eyes fixed on the TV aerial on the roof of your house?

b. wrap your arms round his waist and hold him as tightly as you possibly can without actually stopping him *breathing*?

c. rest your hands loosely on his shoulders, close your eyes, and hope and pray your dad's not about to take Fido out for his last walkies of the day?

10

3. How many boys have you ever kissed — approximately? (Practice makes perfect, after all.)

a. Two, counting your brother who you kiss every year on his birthday.

b. Eleven, so far. You know, 'cos you keep a record of them at the back of your diary!

c. You keep losing count when you get to thirty.

4. You're at a pretty boring party, and to liven things up, someone suggests going back to your childhood (remember, when parties lasted from 6-9 p.m.?), and having a game of postman's knock — just for a laugh, ho ho. Would you . . .

a. most likely be the one who suggests it?

b. wait for a few tactful minutes then suddenly say all that Coke's made you feel sick and you have to go, immediately?

c. grin and bear it? Then, when you have to go outside for a snog with the nice-looking guys, make the most of it; but when you land up with the creeps, laugh and say, all superior-like, "Isn't this ridiculous? As if anybody's actually going to *kiss* out here!"

5. What d'you think of kissing, in general?

a. Seems pretty daft, but if you want a guy to ask you out again you've got to do it, so you might as well try to enjoy it.

b. It's what your lips are for, innit?

c. The longer you can put it off, the better; why, it just *kills* intelligent conversation!

6. Last weekend, you got off with a new guy at the disco. Now he's asked you for another date — where, in your experience, is he most likely to want to take you?

a. The fairground, or stock-car racing, or to meet all his mates.

b. For a walk along the canal — it's *very quiet* along by the canal!

c. To the pictures, to see the eighth re-make of "Close Encounters Of The Third Kind," 'cos he's an addict.

7. One of THE most gorgeous, fantastic-looking, sexy, trendy guys in school has asked you to go to a party with him — only, he turns out to be painfully shy and nervous, with obviously not much experience of girls. As everyone else in the room gets stuck into the Big Romantic Scene in earnest, you two sit side by side as if you're at Annie Walker's coffee morning, and all your guy's managing is to make remarks like "Hot in here, isn't it?" and "Good music, that." What d'you do in this situation?

a. Decide you'll have to take the lead — so you slip your hand in his, start telling him how you've fancied him for ages, and soon get on to nibbling his earlobes and sighing deeply.

b. Keep on calling all your mates over for a chat, to keep the conversation going. If *he's* not going to get passionate, neither are you!

c. It just wouldn't happen — 'cos somehow you *always* end up with guys who are very forward and keen to get to know you better — guys with lots of experience and know-how!

8. You're going out with a guy who's sort of *poetic* by nature — he writes songs and sends you little love letters an' soppy things like that. Think about yourself for a minute, then, at a guess, choose which one of these nicknames he'd be most likely to use as his "pet" name for you . . .

a. Little Lamb.
b. Cheeky Chops.
c. Sexy Sadie.

Now add up your score, as follows:

1. a 3. b 1. c 2
2. a 1. b 3. c 2
3. a 1. b 2. c 3
4. a 3. b 1. c 2
5. a 2. b 3. c 1
6. a 1. b 3. c 2
7. a 2. b 1. c 3
8. a 2. b 1. c 3

So, is *your* kiss a moment of bliss?

If you scored between . . .

8-13 Brrr! Ever noticed how, after a few dates with you, most guys come down with a bout of pneumonia? An orange ice-lolly's going to do more to warm a guy up than a smackeroo from *your* chilly chops! Don't worry, though — guys probably fancy you for the way you dance, or the way you talk, or maybe even because you're a very independent, liberated girl who's got no time for silly, soppy things like kissing and cuddling — everybody's got *some* attraction! If you *do* want to raise your kissing quotient, though, just try forgetting where you are, who you are, who's watching, or whatever else is going on in that busy head of yours when a guy's kissing you. Kissing can be *fun*!

14-18 Well, maybe it *does* take you a little while to warm up and get going, but you've certainly had your moments! You're not a girl who's afraid to show her feelings — to the right guy in the right place. Some guys may think you're rather cool — you've probably left some poor bloke wondering if he's using the wrong toothpaste by now! On the other hand, once you've decided that you've met a guy you like, your kisses can be dynamite! You've got your fair share of Pecking Power all right — it's just that you don't throw it around!

19-24 Wow! Ever heard the nickname 'Hot Lips'? — it was invented for you! Ten minutes with you and most guys are probably wondering who turned up the central heating! Some people are just passionate by nature — and you're one of them! Either that or you just believe in making the best of a good thing — 'specially when it's five minutes in the arms of one of your favourite hobbies — boys! Be careful, though — kissing and cuddling are OK, but there *are* other things you can do with guys — like *talking* to them sometimes! You never know, you might enjoy that, too!

I'LL HAVE TO PULL MYSELF TOGETHER. PHIL IS NICE, BUT IF I MAKE ANY MORE DAFT MISTAKES, HE COULD REPORT ME.

My date with Steve was worth all the nerves, though . . .

I'VE HAD A GREAT TIME, THANKS.

MY PLEASURE. AND I'D LIKE TO SEE YOU AGAIN, JILL. HOW ABOUT SUNDAY?

So after that we saw each other regularly, on Steve's nights off . . .

STEVE, I'VE BEEN THINKING, COULDN'T I COME TO THE PUB ONE NIGHT AND WATCH YOU AT WORK?

WHAT? ER—I DON'T THINK SO. I MEAN, YOU'RE STILL UNDER AGE.

YES, BUT I WOULDN'T BE DRINKING ALCOHOL. I'D STICK TO ORANGE JUICE.

NO, I DON'T THINK IT WOULD BE A GOOD IDEA, LOVE. IT DOESN'T DO FOR A DJ TO HAVE A GIRLFRIEND. IF THEY SAW YOU HANGING AROUND, HALF THE GIRLS AT THE DISCO MIGHT STOP COMING.

I felt a bit peeved, though . . .

I'M FALLING FOR STEVE IN A BIG WAY—BUT IT SEEMS AS IF HE'S KEEPING A PART OF HIS LIFE SECRET FROM ME. IT'S NOT FAIR . . .

AND IF THAT HAPPENED, I'D BE OUT ON MY EAR. NO CROWDS, NO JOB.

WELL, OK THEN, STEVE, IF YOUR JOB DEPENDS ON IT . . .

JILL! DID YOU HEAR ME?

WHAT? OH, SORRY, PHIL. WHAT DID YOU SAY?

YOU'RE JUST NOT CONCENTRATING THESE DAYS. IF THE BOSS NOTICES, HE'LL GO BANANAS! YOU'RE STILL ON A TRIAL PERIOD, REMEMBER! WHAT IS IT, ANYWAY? BOYFRIEND TROUBLE?

WELL, YES AND NO.

I'M GOING OUT WITH STEVE TURNER. HE'S THE DJ AT THE CROWN AND FEATHERS.

I KNOW THE ONE. BOY, THEN YOU DO HAVE PROBLEMS. HE ALREADY HAS A GIRLFRIEND!

Continued on page 12

SO WHY DIDN'T YOU FINISH WITH HER?

I STARTED TO GO OUT WITH HER ABOUT SIX MONTHS AGO. I THOUGHT SHE WAS OK, THAT'S ALL. BUT SHE WAS DEAD SERIOUS ABOUT US.

I WAS GOING TO. THEN HER DAD DECIDED TO OPEN THE DISCO. I'D SET MY HEART ON BECOMING A DJ, AND MR SIMONS SAID I'D GET THE JOB— BUT HE MADE IT OBVIOUS THAT IT DEPENDED ON CAROLINE AND ME STAYING TOGETHER. SO I GOT ENGAGED TO HER, JUST TO PLEASE HIM.

BUT ISN'T THAT BEING PRETTY ROTTEN TO CAROLINE? YOU'RE JUST USING HER.

DON'T WORRY, I'LL LET HER DOWN GENTLY WHEN THE TIME COMES. AND SOMETHING TELLS ME IT COULD BE SOON . . .

OH STEVE, YOUR KISSES TELL ME YOU LOVE ME AS MUCH AS I LOVE YOU. IF ONLY THINGS WEREN'T SO COMPLICATED.

I'LL BE ABLE TO APPLY FOR OTHER DJ JOBS SOON, ONCE I'VE GOT A BIT OF EXPERIENCE BEHIND ME . . .

AND THEN ALL THIS LYING WILL BE OVER?

OF COURSE, LOVE. TRUST ME. ALL YOU HAVE TO DO IS WAIT A LITTLE WHILE LONGER . . .

Next day at work, Phil asked how things were going . . .

WELL, STEVE EXPLAINED ALL ABOUT CAROLINE . . .

SO HE'S CHUCKING HER, IS HE?

NOT EXACTLY . . .

I told him the whole story . . .

IT ALL SOUNDS A BIT ROTTEN TO ME. I MEAN, NO MATTER HOW GENTLY HE DOES IT, CAROLINE'S STILL GOING TO GET HURT.

NO, IT WON'T BE LIKE THAT. STEVE DOESN'T WANT TO HURT ANYONE . . .

But though I stuck up for Steve in public, in private I was having my doubts, too . . .

I THINK WE SHOULD TELL CAROLINE WE'RE GOING OUT TOGETHER, RIGHT AWAY. SHE'LL BE UPSET, BUT SURELY SHE'LL UNDERSTAND. AFTER ALL, STEVE AND I COULDN'T HELP FALLING IN LOVE . . .

So I told Steve what I'd decided—but he wasn't very pleased . . .

ARE YOU JOKING? I'VE TOLD YOU, MY JOB DEPENDS ON US KEEPING IT A SECRET. I KNOW HOW YOU FEEL, BUT WE'VE GOT TO DO THIS MY WAY.

Continued on page 16

PUZZLE IT OUT!

Two jigsaw jumpers – one for you, one for your guy – exclusively designed for Patches by Alan Dart. So get busy and knit yourself a warm 'n' woolly winter!

WOOL — Of **Patons Clansman**; 8 (8, 9, 10) 50 gram balls in main colour, 1 ball in light contrast and 1 ball in dark contrast. (1 ball each of light and dark contrast is sufficient if knitting two jumpers.)

NEEDLES — One pair of 3¼ mm and one pair of 4 mm.

TENSION — 22 sts and 30 rows to 10 cms (4 in.) square on 4 mm needles.

ABBREVIATIONS — K — knit; P — purl; st, sts — stitch(es); tog — together; beg — beginning; dec — decrease by knitting 2 sts together; inc — increase by knitting into front and back of stitch; st-st — stocking-stitch, (1 row K, 1 row P); MC — main colour; LC — light contrast; DC — dark contrast.

MEASUREMENTS — To fit *32 (34, 36, 38) in.* bust/chest; length *23 (23½, 24, 24½) ins.;* Sleeve seam *17 (17½, 18, 18½) ins.*

Instructions for larger sizes in brackets.

BACK.
(Both Boy's And Girl's).
With 3¼ mm needles and MC cast on 99 (105, 111, 117) sts and work 20 rows K1, P1 rib.

Change to 4 mm needles and continue in st-st commencing with a K row.*

Work 92 (96, 100, 104) rows.

Shape Armholes.
Cast off 6 (6, 8, 8) sts at beg of next 2 rows.

Dec 1 st at beg of next and every following row until 73 (75, 77, 79) sts remain **.

Continue without shaping until 172 (176, 180, 184) rows have been worked from start.

Shape Shoulders.
Cast off 10 (11, 11, 11) sts at beg of next 2 rows.

Cast off 10 (10, 11, 12) sts at beg of next 2 rows.

Hold remaining 33 sts on a stitch holder.

BOY'S FRONT.
As back to *.

Work 10 rows.

Work pattern thus — K20, K first row of chart A (working shaded sts in LC), K to end.

Continue in this manner, reading K rows from right to left and P rows from left to right, until all 60 rows of chart have been worked.

Work 2 (6, 10, 14) rows MC.

Work pattern thus — K to last 58 (60, 62, 64) sts, K first row of chart B (working shaded sts in DC), K to end.

Continue until 20 rows of graph have been worked.

Shape armholes as back to ** whilst still working from chart.

Continue until all 40 rows of chart have been worked.

32, 34 and 36 in. sizes only — Continue in MC and work 18 rows, ending with a P row.

38 in. size only — In MC continue armhole shaping (4 rows), work 14 rows, ending with a P row.

Divide for neck — K25 (26, 27, 28) sts, slip remaining sts on to a stitch holder.

Next row — Purl.

Next row — Knit.

Next row — P2 tog, P to end.

Repeat the last 2 rows four more times [20 (21, 22, 23) sts.]

Work 10 rows without shaping.

Next row — Cast off 10 (11, 11, 11) sts, K to end.

Next row — Purl.

Cast off remaining 10 (10, 11, 12) sts.

Hold centre 23 sts, rejoin yarn to remaining 25 (26, 27, 28) sts and K to end.

Next row — Purl.

Next row — K2 tog, K to end.

Repeat the last 2 rows four more times [20 (21, 22, 23) sts.].

Work 12 rows without shaping.

Next row — Cast off 10 (11, 11, 11) sts, P to end.

Next row — Knit.

Cast off remaining 10 (10, 11, 12) sts.

GIRL'S FRONT.

As back to *.

Work 20 rows.

Work pattern thus — K to last 60 sts, K first row of chart B (working shaded sts in LC), K to end.

Continue in this manner, reading K rows from right to left and P rows from left to right, until all 40 rows of chart have been worked.

Work 2 (6, 10, 14) rows MC.

Work pattern thus — K18 (20, 22, 24) sts, K first row of chart A (working shaded sts in DC), K to end.

Continue until 30 rows of chart have been worked.

Shape armholes as for back to ** whilst still working from chart.

Continue until all 60 rows of chart have been worked.

Continue in MC and work 8 rows, ending with a P row.

Work neck shaping as for boy's front.

SLEEVES.

With 3¼ mm needles and MC cast on 51 (53, 55, 57) sts and work 20 rows K1, P1 rib.

Change to 4 mm needles and continue in st-st commencing with a K row.

Inc 1 st at beg and end of next and every following 8th (10th, 10th, 10th) row until you have 73 (75, 77, 79) sts.

Continue without shaping until 126 (130, 134, 138) rows have been worked from start.

Shape sleeve head: Cast off 6 (6, 8, 8) sts at beg of next 2 rows.

Next row — K2 tog, K to end.

Next row — P2 tog, P to end.

Next row — Knit.

Next row — Purl.

Repeat the last 4 rows two (one, two, one) more time(s).

Dec 1 st at beg of next and every following row until 23 sts remain.

Cast off.

NECKBAND (All Sizes).

Join left shoulder seam. With 3¼ mm needles pick up 18 sts from right side of neck, 23 sts from centre, 17 sts from left side and 33 sts from back neck (91 sts).

Work 8 rows K1, P1 rib in MC.

Cast off loosely in rib with a 4 mm needle. Sew in all ends.

MAKE UP.

Follow pressing instructions on ball band. Join right shoulder and neck-band seam. Join side and sleeve seams. Sew sleeves into armholes. Press all seams lightly.

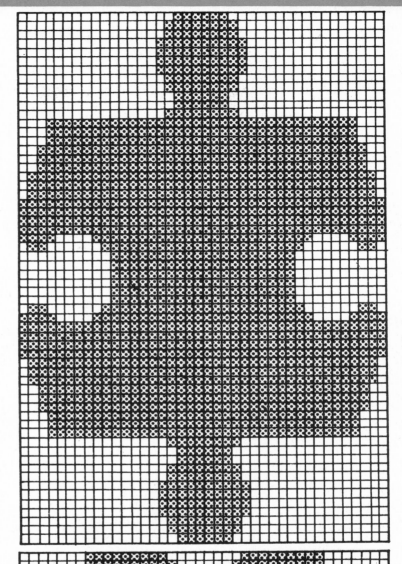

CHART A

CHART B

Continued from page 13

I didn't bother arguing, but afterwards, the nagging doubts continued . . .

IT'S JUST NOT FAIR TO CAROLINE. I'LL HAVE TO PUT MY FOOT DOWN WHEN I SEE STEVE TONIGHT. PERHAPS IF I GO AND SEE MR SIMONS—SURELY HE CAN'T BE AS HEARTLESS AS STEVE MAKES OUT . . .

Then . . .

PHONE FOR YOU, JILL . . .

THANKS MUM.

I HOPE IT'S NOT STEVE CANCELLING OUR DATE, JUST WHEN I REALLY NEED TO TALK TO HIM.

But it wasn't . . .

HELLO, IS THAT JILL? THIS IS CAROLINE—CAROLINE SIMONS. I DON'T KNOW IF YOU KNOW ME, BUT I'M STEVE TURNER'S FIANCÉE.

ER—YES, I–I KNOW ABOUT YOU.

WHAT? YOU MEAN, YOU'VE ARRANGED THE WEDDING?

NOT ME—STEVE. HE WENT ROUND AND SAW THE VICAR HIMSELF, HE'S SO KEEN TO GET MARRIED! STEVE LOVES ME, SO STOP CHASING HIM!

I felt numb as I put down the phone . . .

THEN I DON'T NEED TO GO INTO DETAILS. I THINK IT'S PRETTY ROTTEN TO GO OUT WITH ANYONE WHO'S ENGAGED, BUT IT'S EVEN WORSE WHEN THE WEDDING'S FIXED FOR ONLY A FEW WEEKS AWAY.

STEVE LIED TO ME! HE DOES LOVE CAROLINE, WHATEVER HE SAID. BUT HE OBVIOUSLY CAN'T RESIST STRINGING ANOTHER GIRL ALONG!

Then, the doorbell rang . . .

HELLO GORGEOUS . . .

STEVE! JUST GET OUT OF MY LIFE! I NEVER WANT TO SEE YOU AGAIN!

WHAT? COME ON NOW, I KNOW I'M TEN MINUTES LATE FOR OUR DATE, BUT IS THAT ANY WAY TO TREAT THE GUY YOU LOVE?

I DON'T LOVE YOU! AND WHAT'S MORE, YOU DON'T LOVE ME! YOU NEVER HAVE! I'VE FOUND OUT ABOUT YOUR WEDDING PLANS, STEVE. YOU NEVER INTENDED TO GET RID OF CAROLINE, DID YOU?

NOW, HOLD ON A MINUTE. I CAN EXPLAIN . . .

NO WAY! I'VE HAD ENOUGH OF YOUR EXPLANATIONS! YOU'RE A LIAR AND A CHEAT, STEVE, AND I'M SORRY I EVER MET YOU!

And I slammed the door in his face . . .

THANK GOODNESS HE'S GONE. THAT'S WHAT I SHOULD HAVE SAID TO HIM IN THE FIRST PLACE, WHEN I FOUND OUT HE WAS ENGAGED. POOR CAROLINE—I DON'T ENVY HER ONE BIT . . .

THE END

SHADY LADIES!

Choose your colours — whatever your colouring! It's easy with our step-by-step make-up guide.

Make Up by Jo for Boots 17

1. Tina's make-up free and ready to start.

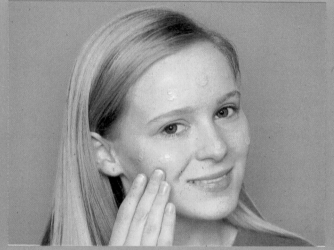

2. Near Skin Foundation in Honey Beige is dotted over her skin. Then Pressed Powder in Translucent to give her face the right base to work on.

3. Blush Powder in Dusty Burgundy shapes her face perfectly.

4. The eyes come next. Deluxe Silky Shadow was used — Blue Stocking for the main shade and Champagne as the highlighter, with Thicklash Mascara in Very Brown for long 'n' lovely lashes.

5. Gleamer lipstick in Poppyfield finishes Tina's make-up off perfectly.

1. Debbie's ready and waiting for her make-up!

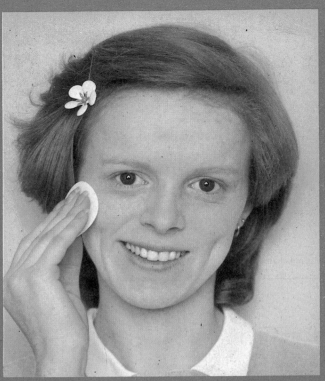

2. After putting on Take Cover foundation in Honey Beige, Pressed Powder in the Translucent shade goes on. Then the Deluxe Shimmering Blush Compact in Rosy Beige Frost helps to accentuate her cheekbones.

3. On to the eyes now. The main shade is Eye Tones in the Brown Tones colour. The highlighter is from the Singles range in Mellow Yellow. Long 'n' Lasting Eye Stix in Bronzed Wood lines the eyes.

4. Making her lips lovely with the Deluxe Colour Performance Lipstick in Cairo Crimson.

5. The finished product — and what a difference!

1. Sharon's ready and raring to go!

2. Hide those spots with a Hideaway Stick in the Fair colour. This is followed by a Take Cover foundation in Natural Beige. Cream Blusher in Toffee Cream completes her foundation.

3. Jo used the singles range for the eyes. The main colour is Coconut Shy, outer edges are Portofino, and Fireglow was used as the highlighter.

4. Make those lashes long and thick with Deluxe Creamy Mascara in Caviar Black.

5. Lips look luscious with Lipgloss in Coffee Caramel.

6. The final picture and Sharon's looking great!

ALL THAT GLITTERS

If you've got some plastic hair-combs, bangles and a pair of sunglasses you're a bit fed up with, here's how you can jazz them up and slay all your mates down at the disco!

All you need is a bottle of clear nail varnish, and a tube of glitter in whichever colour you fancy. Gold or silver glitter show up really well on brightly-coloured plastic, but if the jewellery you have is gold or silver coloured, then try using red or green glitter.

Simply paint the nail varnish on to the bracelet or comb, working quickly so it doesn't dry, then shake some glitter on top. Shake off any excess, leave to dry, then apply another coat or two of nail varnish on top to protect the glitter.

DESPERATE for something new to wear — but no money to buy it with? Don't despair — Patches is here! We've come up with some great ideas for revamping the clothes you have already but are maybe just a little bit bored with.

THE GOLDEN TOUCH

If you've got a pair of worn-out old pale-coloured moccasins lurking in the back of your wardrobe which have been there since the summer before last, don't throw them out. Give them a new lease of life by spraying them gold! We used Dylon Gold Spray.

You'll need to remove any surface dirt and old polish by using Dylon Conditioner and Cleaner, then simply spray your shoes gold! They'll be great for parties!

DENIMANIA!

If you've got a denim jacket you're fed up of (or a friendly brother or boyfriend who does) here's how you can make it look really great and be the envy of all your mates. All you need is a packet of large, round, silver or gold four-pronged studs, and lots of time and patience!

If you've got a good eye, you can start putting the studs on straight away, working in close diagonal lines as shown. Or you can draw in guide lines in chalk if you don't trust yourself to do a straight line! As you can see, you can use the studs on a webbing belt, too. It really makes these belts look special and will match your jacket. We used large ones with smaller ones in between for the belt. You could use the studding technique on a denim shirt if you don't have a jacket — you'll need about 100-150 to cover the whole yoke of the jacket, back and front.

PRETTY VESTS

You can get some very pretty, cheap vests in large department stores which almost look too good to hide under other clothes — so don't! With a tin of dye and some ribbon you can transform a plain white vest into something special for discos.

Choose the colour you'd like — bright pink, yellow and orange usually turn out very well, and dye the vest following the instructions on the tin of dye. This done, you can make the vest even prettier by buying some ½-inch-wide ribbon and sewing it round the neck of the vest. Do this by folding the ribbon in half and pinning one half to the front of the vest, the other half to the back, then sew through both sides on a machine or using long running stitches all the way round. To add an extra special touch you could buy a lace appliqué and dye it at the same time as the vest, then just stitch it on to the front, as shown here. Happy sewing!

A WALK IN THE PARK

A short story by Mary Hooper.

It was just an ordinary, boring old day – until Rufus came along. Then I just *knew* something exciting would happen . . .

I WAS fed up. Everyone — at least everyone who mattered — was away on a school trip, skiing in some place with a funny name in Switzerland. I was practically the only person in the whole world who wasn't there, and I couldn't help feeling just the tiniest bit cheesed off about it. I knew Mum and Dad couldn't really afford it, and I knew we were going abroad ourselves in the summer, but that didn't make it any better.

Right then, sitting coldly in the park, huddled miserably into last year's anorak, I was fed up. They'd be having a fantastic time over there, getting off with the boys from the local college who had also gone, while I just mouldered away.

I desperately wished something exciting would happen so that when they came back, all full of themselves, I could knock 'em dead with what had happened to *me*.

It wasn't on, though, because exciting things didn't happen to me — Miss Average, average height and average face, with average sort of mousey hair.

As I sat there, feeling cross, someone licked my hand. Don't get excited, it wasn't some fantastic guy in shining armour, or even Sting, but a dog. A nice sort of dog, actually. A big, bouncy, red-setter sort of dog.

"Hello," I said in surprise, and the dog put his head to one side and twitched his ears, as if he was saying "Hello" back.

"Nice doggie," I said, and he immediately got up on the bench next to me.

I looked round, but there was no sign of a likely-looking dog-owner, so I put my arm casually over his back. Now, if I owned a dog like this, my life would be so different. I could take him for his walks every day, meeting interesting people (like boys) on the way, attend dog training classes (more boys) and put him in dog shows (even more boys!). I would be known as Kate, that interesting, lively girl with the red setter, instead of boring old average Kathy who only owned a budgie.

I wondered what the dog's name was. "Charles?" I tried, thinking i

ought to be something a bit royal-sounding, and he lifted one eyelid. "Rex?" — He closed it again. "Samuel? Rover? Rufus?" At this last one he lifted both eyelids and gave a little wuff of recognition. Of course — Rufus the Red!

"Walkies, Rufus?" I said experimentally, and he sprang right up and looked at me, dancing about on his doggie toes. I got to my feet. Today, I was someone. Today, I was a dog-owner.

I ran across the grass and Rufus ran beside me, his coat bobbing and gleaming in the few weak rays that the sun was trying to throw. I thought we must look quite a picture, me racing along with my hair streaming out behind me and Rufus gambolling at my side. A girl and her dog — what a pity there wasn't anyone there to see us.

"Here, boy!" I said, and I ran into a clump of bushes and out the other side. Bits of bush stuck to me but I didn't care — when you're a carefree, sporty sort of girl, these things don't matter. I found a few sticks and threw them, and Rufus and I raced after them together.

We were both puffing and panting when we reached the gates on the far side of the park, so I flung myself on to the nearest bench to get my breath back. Rufus lay alongside me, his head on my feet. He had obviously been desperate for exercise. He probably belonged to an old lady who never took him for walks.

A SHADOW fell across us. "What a fantastic dog!" a voice said.

I looked up to find a boy smiling down at me. See, it was true. You only had to get a dog and they came flocking around you.

I smiled back. "Yes, he's super, isn't he?"

"What's his name?"

"Rufus."

"Rufus the Red. I get it."

I smiled again. As well as being extremely good-looking he was obviously a person of some intelligence.

"I expect dogs like that need a lot of exercise."

"Oh, they do," I said readily, trying to pick at least a few of the bits of bush off my clothes. I tried to think of something else to say to him — something which didn't involve dogs and their doings. I could come unstuck if I wasn't careful.

"What does he eat?"

"Er . . . this and that — you know . . . dog food," I said, and then I added very quickly before he had time to ask anything else: "I haven't seen you round here before. Are you visiting someone?"

CONTINUED OVERLEAF

23

FUNNY FARM

CONTINUED FROM PREVIOUS PAGE

"We moved in two days ago," he said, "we're from London."

"Oh," I said. "Stopping long?"

I held my breath after that one, in case he said a week or even less! He had lovely brown eyes which matched Rufus's. Fancy discovering a dog and a new boy all in one day — *and* finding him before he'd got snaffled up by anyone else. I was suddenly glad they were all away.

"Ages. Forever, I should think."

That was all right, then. I ruffled Rufus's fur. "We were just going to walk back across the park," I said. "Care to join us?" Dog owners can afford to be bold. They can pretend that they think the boy is more interested in the dog than them. 'Course, secretly they're hoping all the time that he isn't.

"Great," he said, and we started walking together across the grass, with Rufus running in front of us and every now and then coming back to be patted or to have a stick thrown for him. Quite a picture we must have made. An even better picture than the one before.

I found out lots of things about him, the most important being that his name was Mike and he didn't know a

single other soul, apart from me, in the whole area. I was just about to ask him if he wanted a conducted tour of the town's points of interest when an awful thought struck me.

WHAT was I going to do with Rufus when we got to the other side of the park? I could hardly take him home — Mum would have a fit. Besides, his owner probably had the police out looking for him right now. On the other hand, what would Mike think if I just abandoned him in the park?

By the time we'd reached the park gates I'd thought of two solutions:
1. Confess to Mike that I wasn't an interesting, sporty dog-owner at all and had merely been having him on, or —
2. Fall down in a dead faint.

I was just about to drop gracefully to the ground when Mike said: "We really ought to put Rufus on a lead when we take him out of the park," and he felt around his neck for a collar — something I hadn't even thought of doing.

As he bent over him he said in a surprised sort of voice: "It says here that his name's Samantha!"

I thought quickly. "He's my little

brother's dog and he calls him Samantha, but I don't like the name so I —" my voice tailed away into nothing and I looked at Mike, feeling my face going all hot and pink.

He started laughing. "I've got an awful confession to make," he said.

"So have I," I said sadly. Now he would go away and I'd never see him again.

"Samantha's mine!"

I made a strangled sort of noise in my throat.

"I know I should have told you straight away but you looked so nice sitting there together," he said apologetically, "and you obviously wanted me to believe that she was yours, so I just let you carry on."

I made another strangled noise.

"So, since you like her so much, how about having a share in her?" he went on. "You can come out with us when we go for walks, if you like. Maybe you could show me around the place a bit, too."

I bent down to pat Rufus/Samantha and my face was as red as her fur.

"That would be lovely," I mumbled.

Well, half a dog was better than no dog at all — and half a dog and *Mike*! I couldn't wait for the others to come back! ●

24

BRIGHTEN UP YOUR BEDROOM

FED up with your boring old bedroom but not much money to spend on it? Read on for a few cheap and easy (well, quite easy) ways to make your bedroom the envy of your friends!

The first thing is to think of your room as not just a place to rest your weary head at night, but as your own secret haven away from the rest of the world. The next step is to make it look that way!

First of all, if you haven't had your bedroom decorated for quite a while, maybe you could talk Mum and Dad into buying some paint and paper of your choice. Primary colours such as red, yellow and blue are great for brightening the place up, using white as the accessory colour to cool them down a bit!

If funds don't run to that, though, here are a few things you can do yourself to make your bedroom into a bedsit — a place for entertaining friends, not just sleeping.

MEMO BOARD

This is very useful for recording all those important dates! An easy way to make one is to scout around the stores for a few cork tiles or find somewhere which sells them singly. You can use one for a small memo board, two or four for a large one. All you do is get a piece of cardboard slightly larger than the size you want your memo board to be, glue the tile or tiles on to it then paint a border round the edge of the cardboard using a bright colour. Now attach a strong piece of string to the back of the board with Sellotape and hang it up! Now you're ready to pin all those important notes and letters to it!

There are lots of other bits and pieces, like the memo board, which can add interest to your room — you could buy one of those large brown jars which people use to make wine in (they're called demi-johns and cost about £1) and fill it with dried grasses and/or feathers; soften the lights by buying a red or orange bulb instead of an ordinary one; look out for jumble sale bargains such as old quilts which can be dyed and look great, collect things like shells, pebbles or stones, arrange them tastefully together, and shine your bedside light on them — they'll look great!

SOFT TOUCH

A simple way of turning a bed into a couch is by pushing it up against a wall and scattering some cushions on it. You can buy small scatter cushions very cheaply in markets and large department stores (approximately four for £1).

Then you'll need some nice material — because you're going to cover them! Look in department stores for remnant bargains — you only usually need ½ metre of material to cover these small scatter cushions. But to make sure, measure the cushion, double the measurement and add about 10 cm (4 inches) to allow for hemming. You'll also need scraps of felt for appliqués and snap poppers to close the cushions.

To make a cushion cover, with wrong side of material facing and material folded in half, hem both sides, leaving enough room to get the cushion in, of course! Turn to the right side and put the cushion in. Now cut off any excess material, leaving enough to fold to the inside to make a hem. This done, attach poppers (three or four should be enough) and that's it!

Now you can appliqué some nice shapes on to it. In our picture we've used some dark blue silk lining material, with silver silk moon and star appliquéd on to it. Then there's a simple red felt heart, and for the third one we've hand-embroidered some lettering on, using simple running stitch. And finally, if you're not too neat at cutting shapes out, you can cheat and buy ready-made appliqués — like this butterfly!

You could also edge the cushions with lace or attach tassels to make them look really professional!

SIMPLE SHELVES

I'll bet that no matter how many shelves you have in your room, you could still do with more. Or maybe you don't have any at all. It's amazing how quickly you accumulate little ornaments and souvenirs that need displaying. Or perhaps you're lucky enough to have a record player but haven't anywhere to put it except on the floor?

The problem is easily solved. Do you know anyone who has been having some sort of building work done and might have some bricks and a plank of wood to spare? If not, if there are any building sites near you where houses are being demolished, go along and ask the workmen if they have any odd bits of wood and a couple of bricks you can have. Or failing all else, your local builder can probably sell you some quite cheaply.

Paint the plank of wood with some bright gloss paint, then lay it across the two piles

of bricks (you can have the bricks as high or as low as you like). If you want to ensure that the bricks will give enough support for, say, a record player or some heavy books, pile them in twos.

DREAM LOVER

HEY—WATCH IT!

YOU WANNA HANG ABOUT FOR EVER?

WELL, THANKS VERY MUCH—I DON'T MIND HAVING THE DOOR SHUT IN MY FACE!

How different it would have been in the olden days . . .

AFTER YOU, MISS—NICE WEATHER WE'RE HAVING FOR THE TIME OF YEAR!

YES, SIR. THANK YOU, SIR, BEING A TYPEWRITER IS SO TIRING AT THE END OF A BUSY DAY!

A TYPEWRITER WAS WHAT A TYPIST WAS CALLED IN THOSE DAYS— AND THEY WERE ALWAYS BEING SWEPT OFF THEIR FEET BY SOME SIR GALAHAD . . .

. . . BUT SOME DAY, MY PRINCE CHARMING WILL COME ALONG. HE'LL BE KIND AND GENTLE—TOTALLY DIFFERENT FROM THE BOYS I KEEP MEETING . . .

Take last week, at the disco . . .

DANCIN'?

OK—THANKS . . .

. . . SO I THOUGHT TO MYSELF, IT'S THE DIFF, BUT ON THE OTHER HAND, COULD BE PISTON RINGS, AND I . . .

YES, I SEE . . .

WHO NEEDS SLEEPING PILLS WITH HIM AROUND?

I didn't hear another word. I drifted miles away . . .

SHALL WE DANCE OUT ON THE BALCONY? THE MOON'S RISING ABOVE THE JACARANDAS.

OH, I'D LOVE TO—SOON IT WILL SPREAD THE SEA WITH SILVER.

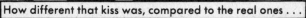

How different that kiss was, compared to the real ones . . .

Like last night's . . .

CHIPS ALMOST DONE THEN?

YES . . .

Continued on page 30

OFF WITH IT!

The extra weight you're carrying around we mean!

We'll show you how.

WE'RE always getting letters from our readers saying they're too fat and how can they get thin.

Well, first of all, not many under-sixteen-year-olds are really fat, and just because your friend is like a bean-pole doesn't mean you have to be the same.

Probably — and highly likely — your friend has a different rate of metabolism from you. Without getting too technical, this basically means her body burns up the food she shovels into it much faster than yours! There's nothing you can do about this and it means your friend will simply always be a thin person.

Having said that, if you get breathless going up stairs, and you can't see your toes easily, far less touch them, you could probably do with losing a few pounds.

The way to do this is to get the calorie intake you need per day from food *right*. The second way is to exercise. And the *third* way is to go on a diet!

But one thing at a time. The easiest way to work out how many calories you need to keep you at your correct weight is to take that weight and multiply it by fifteen. So if you weigh 8 stones 4 pounds (which is 116 pounds) you multiply that by fifteen and come out at the magical figure of 1740 calories, which is all you have to get through in a day to keep you slim 'n' sylph-like!

Now for the nasty bit! One meal, made up of egg, beans and chips, washed down with a cup of milky tea containing *one* sugar, and followed by a *small* doughnut equals — 2580 calories!

Now you don't need to be Master-mind to work out that on one meal alone, you've noshed your way through 840 calories more than you need for an entire day! Therefore, if your jeans are feeling a bit tight and you puff and pant every time you run for a bus — it's your own fault!

In order to get rid of just those extra 840 nasty little fat-making things, you would have to walk at a *very* brisk pace round the block for two and a half hours! If you want to walk round the block for that length of time, then that is entirely your business! You may be very fond of your block!

But an easier way to keep your calorie count and your weight down might be to take up eating hard-boiled eggs!

According to one dietician, a hard-boiled egg consists of 80 calories. But eating it actually uses up 92 calories — which means by the time you've actually got through it, you've lost 12 calories! So, if you could chew your way through 70 boiled eggs a day (ugh!), in theory you'd wind up losing those 840 calories you put on on your eggs, beans and chips binge!

Personally, we'd rather join you in trotting round the block!

HOWEVER, enough of this foolishness! What you need is sensible eating, coupled with at least four intensive sessions at the disco every week!

A grapefruit without sugar for breakfast, plus a cup of black coffee, 1 ounce of brown bread and quarter of an ounce of butter is 138 calories, and a great deal better for you than an enormous fry-up. And even if you're super slim and have bacon and eggs every morning, try this for a change — it's much better for your skin and hair.

If you *must* have the fry-up and you're not super slim, then you're going to have to run all the way to work, or spend half an hour jumping yourself into knots with a skipping-rope, eat nothing but lettuce for the rest of the day (because it's another one like the boiled eggs — it takes so much energy to digest, you start losing weight), or invest in an extremely large dog who needs a ten-mile walk morning and evening!

So set yourself a sensible course.

Cream cakes are fattening — therefore reserve 'em as a treat for special occasions, or have one at the weekend if you honestly haven't chewed chips all week!

If you find yourself cheating and sneaking into shops when everybody's backs are turned — punish yourself! Have a cold bath! By the time you've got into it, splashed about

in it and got out — you'll be shivering so much those extra pounds'll practically wobble themselves off!

Alternatively, if Mum is threatening you with a full roast beef, two veg. and mound of Yorkshire-type Sunday lunch — grab yourself a lot of raw celery sticks, or carrot strips and munch your way through them first.

You'll still eat your lunch — of course you will! You just won't eat quite so *much* of it — because you will be full up with raw carrot, celery, etc.!

Bear in mind, whenever a raw vegetable and you come into contact — that poor, inoffensive veg. is actually a very cheap beauty aid, because it won't give you spots or a greasy skin or lank hair or bulges in the wrong places!

Vegetables are friends! They give you clear skin, shining hair, sparkling eyes and a fairly slim figure. Well,

how many fat vegetarians have you ever seen???

However, if you're reading this and eating a Mars bar instead of nibbling on a nice healthy turnip, the chances are you're hooked on food and need help!

There *are* ways you can throw away the Mars bar.

NEXT time you go to buy yourself a new outfit, try on the size you were wearing last year! If you can still fit into that size,

you're OK. If you have to take a size down, you're on the right road. If you need a size up, dash out of there and stock yourself up with a whole load of hard-boiled eggs! Alternatively, if you like it, can afford it and don't really need it at the moment — buy it, and hang it up on the front of the wardrobe as an awful reminder of what you've got to start doing to yourself!

Falling in love is also great for losing weight! Apart from anything else, right at the beginning when you've just met someone new, you *want* to look your best for him, so you start with the pear, cottage cheese and lettuce syndrome! (If you eat this sprinkled with lemon juice three times a day, you *should* lose 3 to 5 pounds in three days, but only if you don't cheat!)

Then, once you've started going out with him and everything in the garden's coming up snowdrops — you spend such a lot of time on your own worrying about whether he *really* cares, whether he's still seeing his old girlfriend, whether he actually *was* working late the night he told you he was — you burn up a whole lot of energy, and energy is calories! (The other great thing about falling in love is you're so anxious to *be* with him all the time you start running everywhere — and that does wonders, too!)

Of course, there are *other* sensible ways to keep those extra pounds at bay.

A weekly work-out at a gym or dance-class keeps you in shape. So does swimming. So does going along to a sauna — pounds drop off in minutes as you sit panting in all that steam wondering why you were mad enough to come!

Unfortunately, because it's mainly fluid you're losing — they start to go on again the second you stagger out of there and swallow a glass of cold water!

ANY sort of animal is a great weight-watcher. Dogs are the best ones, of course, because you tend to get so hypnotised watching the goldfish just swimming round in circles, you reach out for the nearest gooey cake! Though goldfish *do* have their uses!

One guy we know trimmed his waistline terrifically because his girlfriend had insisted on putting her two fish in a *very* large tank. Every time he took it into the bathroom to change the water, the effort of bending and stretching between spots along the way — because the weight was so much he had to have a rest or his arms would fall off — did wonders for him!

Kittens are quite a snappy idea as well — particularly if you've got a back garden you won't want them to get out of! The exercise involved in climbing up fences and trees to

rescue the darn thing slims you down just about everywhere!

But the *main* thing about staying in shape is to stick to the old saying "moderation in all things." And that means moderating your intake of fattening foods — but it also means moderating your dieting! Extremes of

eating are actually diseases. Really gorging yourself all the time, or "bingeing," is called bulimia nervosa. And dieting when you're far too thin already is anorexia nervosa. Both of them need medical treatment and can take a very long time to "cure." So beware!

Regular exercise is needed to keep you healthy, anyway. And the occasional hard-boiled egg won't do you any harm — you'll be able to feel a glow of achievement every time you eat one, knowing you've just lost twelve calories!

So don't just sit there feeling sorry for yourself! Get those extra pounds off — now!

The Cat's Whispers

Just call me Kit Richard!

Continued from page 27

YOU CAN SQUARE UP WITH ME AFTER—NO HURRY.

OH—YES—OF COURSE.

I gave him the benefit of the doubt . . .

STUDENTS NEVER HAVE A LOT OF MONEY. I SUPPOSE THEY'RE USED TO GOING DUTCH.

At the interval . . .

ANOTHER THIRTY PENCE FOR YOUR ICE —OK?

Y- YES, ALL RIGHT.

It was raining when we came out . . .

HOPE YOU DON'T MIND ME HOGGING THE BROLLY. JUST HAD MY HAIR RESTYLED, YOU SEE.

N- NO, IT'S OK, I DON'T MIND . . .

He was no Sir Walter Raleigh anyhow. If it had been Neville instead of him all those years ago . . .

NICE OF YOU TO LET ME BORROW YOUR CLOAK, MY LADY—SAVES GETTING MY NEW BOOTS MUDDIED.

Y- YES, I'M SURE . . .

WELL, REALLY!

We went for a coffee . . .

BOUND TO GET AN HONOURS DEGREE AT LEAST.

HE TALKS ABOUT HIMSELF ALL THE TIME—OH, I'M NEVER GOING TO FIND MY SIR GALAHAD . . . NEVER!

Then on the way home . . .

NIGHT'S YOUNG. NO HURRY TO GET HOME, IS THERE?

ER—WELL, ACTUALLY I SAID TO MUM . . .

ERGH—I'D RATHER BE KISSED BY THE BOY WITH THE VINEGARY BREATH!

I tried to break away . . .

LET ME GO!

. . . NOW NOW—THAT'S NOT NICE! NOT AFTER A GREAT EVENING LIKE WE'VE HAD.

But I managed to push him off—and then I just ran . . .

HEY, COME BACK! HEY . . .

NO WAY!

OOOOF!

SOMETHIN' THE MATTER?

WELL—UM—ER, MY FRIEND AND I JUST FORGOT TO SQUARE UP FOR THE CINEMA AND THE COFFEES.

SO THAT SHOULD COVER EVERYTHING. GOODBYE!

FINE—NO HASSLE! SEE YOU . . .

NOT IF I CAN HELP IT, CREEP!

BELIEVES IN GETTING HIS POUND OF FLESH, HUH?

YOU COULD SAY THAT—WITH BONUSES.

We discovered we lived quite near each other and started walking home . . .

I SUPPOSE SOME GUYS DO BELIEVE IN SHARING EVERYTHING, BUT I'M THE OLD-FASHIONED TYPE—A DATE'S ALWAYS SOMETHING SPECIAL TO ME. I LIKE TO TREAT A GIRL WHEN I TAKE HER OUT . . .

MAYBE THAT'S WHY I'M BROKE HALF THE TIME—THE NAME'S ARTHUR KING, BY THE WAY.

RONA RUNCIE. PLEASED TO MEET YOU.

KING ARTHUR—AS IN THE ROUND TABLE. THAT FIGURES! I'VE THE FEELING I'VE SEEN HIM SOMEWHERE BEFORE . . .

YOU WOULDN'T LIKE TO COME OUT WITH ME SOME NIGHT . . . WE COULD GO TO THE ICE SHOW AND THEN HAVE A MEAL SOMEWHERE!

THAT WOULD BE JUST ABOUT PERFECT.

IT'S HIM—HE'S THE BOY I'VE BEEN WAITING FOR—MY PRINCE CHARMING.

. . . but I just couldn't remember where I'd seen him before. Could it have been in my dreams?

32

THE END

IT'S TIME TO PUT ON MAKE-UP...

"... it's time to light the lights." These lines should sound pretty familiar to all you Muppet fans out there, but do you ever wonder what the Muppets are like **under** the make-up? We think they must be pretty like us so now we're giving you a chance to find out what **you're** really like by . . . but, who better to explain it all than Mr Presenter himself – Kermit the Frog!

EHM, OK then folks, this is Kermit — of the frog variety — here, and although it has never been my pleasure to conduct a Patches Fun Feature before I'll, eh, do my best. What about if you, eh, sort of select your favourite Muppet and then have a look at how I've described them and that'll give you a pretty good idea of what you're like, too? OK, here we go, descriptions — warts and all! That's a sort of frog joke — perhaps you didn't like it? Never mind . . .

Ehm, for reasons I can only give as personal, I think I should start off with the real star of the show — the glamorous, the gorgeous, the incredible *Miss Piggy!* Yayyy. I think I should also whisper so that I can tell the whole truth about her! Right, first on the list is that she really only likes to hear good things said about herself — taking criticism is *not* her strong point. She likes her own way a lot — well, that's not really true. She likes her own way all the time! And if she doesn't get it, she gets violent and really beats people (and frogs) up! In fact, she hates any kind of reference to animal species that makes them sound inferior; especially if it's things like, "You pig!" or "You big, fat pig!" — in fact, anything with "pig" in it that doesn't also contain the word "beautiful"! Oh, hey, and she also puts words into people's mouths, like imagining that certain frogs have made promises to be true to her and such. In fact, when I think about it, if you're like Miss Piggy, you're gonna be real difficult to live with and you're not gonna have many frog friends at all . . . But that won't bother you, 'cos *people'll* love you (for some reason)!

Now we come to the show's comic interest — well, *somebody* must find it interesting — Mr *Fozzie Bear.* Uh, well, what can I say about old Fozzie? Well, he tries really hard all the time. And he's always coming up with ideas for the show — and even though they don't

work, it doesn't matter too much. Oh, and he tells jokes all the time. Well, he has to, because that's his job — it's just that he's not very good at it. Oh, and he's really always willing to help a guy out of a tight spot; the fact that he usually makes things worse — well, I suppose that's really neither here nor there, is it? Fozzie has to be one of our most loveable employees, and he's kind, and he just wants to help everyone and he's very sensitive and he wouldn't hurt a fly — so why is it he drives me mad? I don't know, perhaps you people who are always bending over backwards to be the nice guy all the time, and never say anything bad about anybody, and always want to be everybody's pal, just get to a stage where you become

utterly sickening! Wait a minute, guys — I'm only joking, honest! Fozzie's looking over my shoulder, so it wouldn't do to write anything *nice* about him, now would it?

Yes, well, now, I think I'd better pass on quickly to Muppet number three. *Animal!*

Now, I, eh, well, I must admit that, weird though Animal is, I have a kinda soft spot for him. It's, uhm, when he looks at you with those little, crazy eyes — gets to me every time, sorta cute. And he's dedicated, know what I mean? Anything can be going on around Animal in this crazy place and he'll still come up with that old drum-roll at the right time, amazing really. In fact, I suppose if Animal has a fault, it's that he's a little **too** dedicated to his art; he really is very easy-going until anybody says anything about his drumming and then he's likely to go berserk if it doesn't match up with his ideas. Still, you do have to make allowances for the artistic temperament — like that time he wrecked the stage and broke . . . yeah, well, enough about that!

Now, let me tell you about *Rowlf the Pianist.* Y'know, he's been

ROWLF
ANIMAL
SWEDISH CHEF
FOZZIE BEAR
KERMIT
MISS PIGGY

around the theatre for longer than I care to remember and never a harsh word for anyone. Really, you folks out there, if you like Rowlf best in the show, it's a real credit to you. See, not too many people really even notice him at all. Well, he's kinda quiet and unassuming, isn't he? Just gets on with the job. And he's talented, too, y'know! Rowlf does an awful lot of those arrangements himself. What I really have to say about Rowlfie Baby is that the boy's a *Pro*fessional through and through. I should say that, if you like Rowlf you're probably a little like him

yourself, always ready to help out, always remembering to do little, important things for other people and getting on with it quietly and with a smile — yup! that's Rowlf for you, yessir!

I guess there's quite a few of you out there keen on the gourmet spot as well and that kinda brings us to the **Swedish Chef.** Well, gee, I don't really know what to say about the guy who cooks. You have to understand that I'm not really qualified to say too much about him on the basis that I don't *know* too much about him! It's not that I haven't *tried* but it can't have escaped your notice that he doesn't, uhm, speak too good — not like us frogs. I can't get past the "Oh, scordey-gloop!" It sounds friendly enough, but then you can't tell with these foreigners, can you? Put that with the fact that he's a top-class chef (or so he told me) and you'll realise he can be pretty temperamental. That's something you have to accept in show-business, but what really gets to me, and I know I shouldn't be saying this, is that the guy is really *messy.* Maybe that's why people like him, because they're messy, too? And those hens, the little "chickie-doos" — have you noticed that they're always *alive* when he throws them in the pot? I've heard of people doing that with lobsters, but hens?! Mind you, folks, he has what we in the trade call charisma. He may not make too many edible dishes but he sure as heck keeps you entertained while he's doing it!

And to round things off in this little celebrity feature, I'd like to talk about — last but not least by any means — cute, little green frogs called Kermit! That was actually a sort of joke. I used to want to be a stand-up comic — never quite had the nerve to do it, though. Suppose that's why I really do admire old Fozzie Bear; all of them, actually. I mean, I know I have to be here and shout at them all, and I make a really big production out of that, but it's only because really, deep down, I wanted to be out there in the spotlight myself with everyone rooting for me. Oh, don't get me wrong — I've met all these great guys through my job, and lots of verrry nice ladies, too, but it's not the same as being a star. I knew I could never make it so that's why I took this job; next best thing to actually being out there among the footlights. Sometimes I sit here in the empty theatre, after they've all gone home, and I think what a failure I really am — wonder why I was the one who never made it . . . ''

And, as the curtain goes down on the sad, little figure, we realise that he could've been the best actor in the world if he'd wanted to be!

There it is, then — a run-down of the Muppets, and you have to believe that whichever is your favourite is the one you're most like. Did you recognise yourself? Fortunately, it's all for fun, so don't get too upset, all you Miss Piggies!

33

HOW TO BE A

WHAT with Pyjama Parties, Hen Parties and Coming-Out Parties, not to mention Arty Parties, Smarty Parties and The Conservative Party, it's difficult nowadays to know just what kind of party to throw for your friends.

Well, we hope we'll be able to help, by suggesting various kinds of party that you and your friends might be able to organise.

For example, there's **THE BORING PARTY.** Now, this kind of party might sound a little tedious, but don't let that fool

to provide boring little extras like dry toast spread with crackers, or Weetabix-on-a-stick.

A little more light-hearted perhaps, is the **BLACK AND WHITE PARTY.** Your multi-racial guests must all come wearing only black and white, but Nun's Habits and Zebra skins should be discouraged.

Unless someone can play the piano keys, music will be restricted to Two-Tone records — Specials, etc., until exhaustion of the legs sets in. After that, Al Jolson's version of

parties of all are the **ONE-TO-ONE PARTIES.** Simply invite the fanciable guy you've had your eye on for ages, and tell him he's going to be the only guest. With something smoochy on the record player, something tasty on the table, and something saucy on the sofa, you can expect a wonderful evening.

The advantages of this kind of party are — a) you don't have any shortage of fellas, b) you don't have any surplus of females, c) you don't have any trouble finding someone to dance with, and d) you don't have to stand in a queue for twenty minutes every time you want to go to the loo. Unless your guy is particularly fussy when it comes to brushing his hair!

you, because actually it's **extremely** tedious! Invite as many of the most boring people you know as possible and you're in for an event of mind-numbing monotony. With everyone bopping away to the sounds of Des O'Connor and Max Bygraves on a Sunday afternoon, what more could you ask?

There are lots of appropriate boring-party games that can be played, like Blindfold Charades. This is just like ordinary Charades, except that as well as not being allowed to speak, everyone has to wear a blindfold while trying to guess what film/book/song title is being acted out. However, we must warn you that this can prove to be a very long game. Much shorter is Hunt-The-Grand-Piano, an easier version of Hunt-The-Thimble.

As far as food is concerned, bread and water is usually all you'll need, but you may wish

horrible little Nibbley Bits →

White Christmas can be played for the rest of the party.

Food poses few problems for the imaginative hostess. Badger-burgers, Panda-meat paste on biscuits and liquorice sandwiches should go down well. As far as what to drink is concerned, Guinness and milk shandies will prove popular.

Games include ducking-for-snowballs - in - a - basin - of - ink, and let's get-the-stains-out-of-Mum's-new-rug, as well as the quieter one of dominoes.

We recommend that these parties are always well-lit. Alan once spent two hours in the dark chatting up a girl at a Black & White Party, and when the lights came on he discovered he'd p-p-picked up a Penguin!

With a bit of luck, the best

We'll leave you to invent your own Party Pieces, but Postman's Knock always proves to be a popular game.

The funny thing about One-to-One Parties is that there still won't be enough chairs, and you'll still have to sit on his lap, squeeze in close, or cuddle up together in a corner.

The **only** disadvantage these parties have is that if your one-and-only guest doesn't turn up, the party usually ends up as a . . .

NO-GUEST PARTY. This is easily the cheapest party to organise, and is the most popular with parents and next-door-neighbours. Take great care in choosing the people you're not going to invite, then don't send invitations to anyone. If you can arrange to be out of the house on the night of the party as well, then it's bound to be a huge success.

PARTY SMARTY!

for dancing, eating, kissing and cuddling – have a Patches party! And if your parents don't strangle you, and your neighbours don't mangle you – you might have fun!

One thing to keep in mind is not to prepare too many snacks, or you'll be eating mini-sandwiches and sausage rolls for the next two months! However, this will be compensated for by the complete absence of cigarette burns in the cushions and crisps trodden into the carpet.

One final word of warning, though. The last No-Guest Party we weren't invited to and didn't go to was completely ruined when a bunch of nobodies gate-crashed half way through and stayed for the rest of the evening!

As far as music is concerned — stick a dinner plate on the stereo. Who's going to notice?

THE BACKWARDS PARTY is an invention of our own that we're rather proud of. Invite yourselves along to the house of someone you've never met, and arrive at two o'clock in the morning. The party will then run until just after tea-time. Stay as quiet as you possibly can for the first hour, then rush down to the flat below and complain that you can't hear their stereo!

The evening before, you'll have spent hours preparing lots and lots of food which you will take along to the party and leave there.

The guests will be announced in reverse order, as they leave, and the only music allowed will be "I'm Walking Backwards For Christmas" by the Goons.

Games are difficult to suggest for a party like this. If the room isn't big enough for Tug-Of-War, then the teams will just have to pull one at a time.

But perhaps you're looking for something a little more conventional? Well, the **DRESSING UP AS FAMOUS PEOPLE PARTY** is as much fun as it sounds. (Yawn!)

All the guests must arrive dressed as a well-known personality. For example, Joe once painted himself green and went as The Incredible Hulk . . . Anne once bleached her hair and went as Debbie Harry . . . and The Ed once turned up wearing his best suit, and won first prize as Worzel Gummidge!

Music is no problem, as there are millions of records by totally unknown singers trying to sound like someone famous.

However, we do not recommend that you "dress up" as the famous Lady Godiva, Adam and Eve, or a page 3 model, because all you'll end up with is a chilly reception, frozen looks, a cold shoulder from the hostess, not to mention a very numb . . . ahem . . .

The best way to melt any icy welcome is to organise a **SNOGGING PARTY!** Traditionally, these parties are for couples only, as kissing yourself can be very monotonous, not to mention extremely painful! (You try nibbling your own ear-lobe and see how far you get!)

Food . . . who needs it!?
Music . . . who cares!?
Unless you have some very

Continued on page 37

35

1982 Starts Here!

What's in store for you in the year ahead? Want a sneak preview? Then take a look at our Patches guide to what the stars say about *you* in '82!

March 21-April 20

Because of your own determination, this could be a year when you really move ahead in a direction you've been dying to follow for ages! On the fella front, someone you haven't thought about for a long time may suddenly come back into your life quite seriously, and you'll be surprised at the changes in him!

April 21-May 20

Your normal easy-going attitude is suddenly going to harden up around your birth-date, and quite a lot of people who've been taking you for granted seem in for a nasty shock! As far as boys are concerned — look forward to meeting someone special during the holiday season, and don't trust someone who approaches you about a friend! He may not be what he seems! You'll be luckiest in July and September.

May 21-June 20

If you'd give up arguing and changing your mind all the time, 1982 could be a terrific year for you! The stars predict a lot of fun times with friends ahead, and there's a possibility of an existing friendship turning into something much deeper. Some time around the middle of the year, you're going to find yourself in a confused emotional state, probably involving two guys, and the choice you make then will influence what happens next.

June 21-July 21

Looks as if your creative side is going to come out on top this year, if you'll stop being so lazy! Exam results, or work prospects, are brighter than they might have been. But where boys are concerned, you *might* be in for a bit of heartache around August. Don't worry! It'll pass! Best time of the year for you will be the spring and late autumn.

July 22-August 21

Being over-generous could get you into hot water around your birthday, and early in the year you're going to have to act quickly in a tricky situation, otherwise it could get out of hand. A special boy seems set to appear on a Sunday that's got a 9 in it, but don't let your heart rule your head! Your own birth month seems to begin a lucky period.

August 22-September 21

Honesty is always going to be the best policy where you're concerned, but you might suddenly find yourself in a situation where it would be wiser *not* to tell the truth! Your own selfishness could wreck a relationship, but apart from that, the fella front will be a satisfying one for you this year. Successful times seem to be January, August and September.

September 22-October 22

Stop daydreaming and come out in the real world! If you do, you're in for a terrific year because everything around you seems to be coming up roses! A close relationship could get even closer, and there seems to be talk of engagements or weddings in the air. *Don't* start changing your mind about relationships in June and July. Carry on as you are until September.

October 23-November 21

Itchy feet are your main problem this year! You want to get up and get on, but things are still holding you back. Keep an eye on your temper — it could lose you friends if it gets out of control. You're going to feel a bit mixed up about someone you didn't even think you liked, but this situation should sort itself out for the better by the beginning of October.

November 22-December 20

Pride comes before a fall, so watch out for yours! This year could see a lot of changes for you, maybe even a move away from home if a career situation is being talked about. People are important to you, and there seem to be three of four guys around in 1982 who are all going to make a considerable impression on you! Your best months are April, May and July.

December 21-January 19

Don't be so easy-going! People are taking you for granted, and *some* people aren't even noticing you're around! This is a year for speaking your mind and actually *doing* things instead of just thinking about them. A holiday romance that starts around August could develop into something deeper, but you might also find it leads to conflict with someone you'll meet at the beginning of May.

January 20-February 18

You seem set to charm the birds off the trees this year, and your social life is definitely on the up and up! February could see what you thought might be a romance settling into a very close *friendship*. But someone you haven't met before appears on the scene in the summer, and there's a chance you could be swept off your feet! Your absolutely best time for taking action on things is going to be April through to July.

February 19-March 20

If you've just gone through some kind of broken romance, don't worry. You'll begin to realise it wasn't actually as serious as you thought. An older bloke comes into the picture about the middle of the year, but be careful. Jealousy on both sides could make the relationship a stormy one! Reason things through before you make any decision, particularly for the two weeks or so after your birthday. Your best month seems to be August, especially if you're taking a seaside holiday.

Had a rough deal from love? Been shuffled about by boys? Fed-up of the whole pack? Find out how you really feel about boys and romance and . . .

Put Your Cards On The Table!

♦ ♠ ♥ ♣ ♦ ♠ ♥ ♣

Take the following playing cards from a pack and lay them face down on the table in any order: King of Diamonds, King of Hearts, King of Clubs, King of Spades, Knave of Diamonds, Knave of Hearts, Ace of Hearts, Ace of Diamonds, Ten of Hearts and Joker.

Let your mind become absolutely blank and pick a card, letting your hand move quickly and instinctively. Now for the moment of truth! Which card did you choose?

KING OF DIAMONDS: You admire success and sophistication and people who know what they're doing and where all the best places to go are. You may be attracted to older guys, seeing them as a kind of status symbol. But you've always got your feminine intuition to stop you getting out of your depth.

KING OF HEARTS: Personality is more important to you than looks, and you realise that a guy doesn't have to be stunning to possess that magic called charisma. You don't expect your guy to be perfect, but so long as he's warm-hearted, generous and affectionate, he's tops with you.

KING OF CLUBS: You're not really ready for romantic involvements yet. What you're looking for is friendship — uncomplicated and sincere. A feeling of security is very important to you, and you can get that with friends.

KING OF SPADES: At the moment you're unhappy about your romance — or the lack of it. Perhaps you're meeting someone in secret or feel you can't trust your guy. Altogether, it's bad news, so take a good look at your relationship. Alternatively, you might just have had a disappointment romance-wise and are still brooding over it. Cheer up, it won't last long!

KNAVE OF DIAMONDS: Looks matter a lot to you, and if a guy isn't wearing the right clothes, he doesn't stand a look in. You tend to go for guys in uniform, and admire them only for their looks.

KNAVE OF HEARTS: It seems too good to be true that a wonderful guy could be interested in you, although deep down you know his affection is sincere. You can't believe your luck and you're living from day to day.

ACE OF HEARTS: You're a one-guy girl and see the boy in your life through rose-tinted glasses. If you don't have a guy just now, you'll almost certainly have picked one out, and once you go to work on him he hasn't got a chance of escaping!

ACE OF DIAMONDS: Admit it! All you're after is an engagement ring to dazzle your friends with. For you, a guy's greatest attraction can be his money.

TEN OF HEARTS: You're a dancing queen and not ready to go steady. You fight for your right to be free to flirt, but may end up breaking a lot of hearts.

JOKER: You don't take boys too seriously, do you? At least, that's what you want them to think. Well, it's great to have a sense of humour, but with you around the most romantic setting is likely to turn into a slapstick comedy. You're secretly afraid that boys only chat you up to take the mickey, but when you stop laughing at them you'll find that they can be sincere, too.

HOW TO BE A PARTY SMARTY!

Continued from page 35

liberated friends, make it quite clear at these Snogging Parties that girls must stick to the partners they came in with. Otherwise, Snogging Parties can be very easily followed by Slapping Parties, Screaming Parties and Eye-blacking Parties!

Which brings us quite nicely to a **SMASHING PARTY**. This doesn't need to be as destructive as it sounds, but it's much more fun if it is. No paper plates, plastic cups or Cookery Class biscuits are allowed. Everything must be breakable.

A list of things liable to get broken at such a party is; glasses, vases, windows, hearts, the dog, LPs, engagements, promises, various ornaments, lights and teeth!

Houses containing valuable antique collections or irreplaceable China Tea Sets are perfect venues for these parties.

As long as everyone enters into the spirit of the thing, Smashing Parties can be smashing fun, but it's advisable that everyone present leaves the country immediately afterwards, before their parents return home . . .

The most amazing thing of all is the way that many quiet, ordinary, normal parties turn into Smashing Parties without really trying at all . . .

Well, after all this excitement, you might need to relax a little, and what better way than by throwing a **SLEEPING PARTY**, with everyone dressed up in their pyjamas, being lullabied by the gentle sounds of Des O'Connor or Max Bygraves (them again!).

No-one is ever in the mood for games, but a Pillow Fight might be organised if you can find two pillows that hate each other enough. The only food you need supply is usually cocoa and chloroform, but by the end of the evening you'll probably find your house is filled with kippers, kipping.

Finally, we'd like to warn you never to organise a **HEN PARTY**. Chickens are terrible kissers, can't dance for toffee, and leave feathers strewn all over the house!

So that's it, except to say that for the best party you'll ever have, invite us all from the office. We'll each bring along a Red Indian friend, a piece of fruit and a dog, and we'll hold the party at Wembley or Anfield or Old Trafford. You must know what that party is called . . .

A PATCHES APACHE'S PEACHES POOCHES AND PITCHES PARTY. What else . . .?

CHAINED-UP CHARLIE AND THE CATERPILLAR KID

A *short story specially written for Patches by Barbara Jacobs.*

Y ET another wet Monday! As I came out of the office that evening, I could hardly see across the road to the bus stop. Rain hung out of the grey city sky like dirty, tattered sheets, and clung to my face and my hair as I made a desperate dash through the traffic. By the time I joined the queue, I felt and looked as if I'd swum ten lengths of Ellis Street Baths, fully dressed. Wet Mondays I could do without.

And *him* I could do without, too. But there he was, miraculously sliding into the queue in front of me, as usual — Charlie Wilson, still haunting me, dripping raindrops and wit.

"Hi, Lucy!" he grinned, with rain ski-jumping from the end of his smug little nose. "You look like a drowned mouse!"

"Rat!" I growled.

"You're too small to be a rat," he jeered.

"I wasn't correcting you — I was making a comment about you!" I jeered back.

"Oh! It's one of *those* Mondays, is it?" he grinned.

"Yeah! And you're the final disaster!" I spluttered, shaking rain from me like a wet dog, hoping he'd dissolve in the spray. "What're you doing hanging round town anyway, night after night? Aren't you still a schoolboy?"

Even that stinging comment didn't deter him. He'd heard it before. I was very self-satisfied about the fact that I'd finally left him and school behind.

"Library," he explained. "Just as well you got a job, Lucy. You have to be able to read to get into the sixth form!"

The bus came before my reply. To be honest, I couldn't think of anything to say anyway. He'd always been able to get the last word in, whenever we started on the cross-talk. Cross-talk's all we ever did, these days. That, and bump into each other, accidentally, all over the place. There seemed to be no way I could get clear of his sudden cheeky grins, or the sharp flash of his eyes.

I really couldn't stand him, especially on wet Mondays when I looked like a drowned mouse and had to steam next to him on a crowded bus, and carry on the fight we'd had for three whole years.

T HREE years ago, we actually fancied each other. I'd been shy and gawky then, and he'd been fantastic-looking, and shy and gawky, too. We'd smiled shyly at each other for months before he made the first gawky move and asked me out. It was the first and last date.

Awful, it was. No, it was worse than awful — it was horrific. He'd been into punk, and I'd been into sleazy glamour, and we'd slid along to the Palais to do the latest dances. He'd been so enthusiastic in his zany leaping about that one of the chains on his jacket swung across my eye, dislodging an experimental false eyelash I'd borrowed from Mum.

He spent the rest of the evenin trying to chain himself up again, and spent it rubbing my red eye. It too him an hour to tell me there was caterpillar crawling along my cheek and ask if I'd trained it specially. removed the eyelash as stylishly as could, held it in the palm of my hand and said to it, "Cuthbert, it's time we went home. This punk's starting t irritate me!"

We didn't speak for a year. Whe we did, it was with reluctance, an only when we had to, in grunts an nods. Now, though, it was open wa with the battles about even.

The rain had died down to a splutte when the bus slurped to a halt at ou stop. We maintained a steamy, we silence all the way to my front gate I didn't want to speak to him at a after he'd made that quip about m stupidity. He'd always put on tha big superior act with me.

"I suppose you'll be coming to th sixth-form disco this week . . ." h muttered as I started to open the gate

"Wouldn't be seen dead with crowd of schoolkids!" I sneered swinging myself on my heel, swingin my bag on to my shoulder in what hoped was a defiant gesture. clonked against the gatepost and burs open, scattering papers, tissues make-up, purse, old earrings, pens bits of chewed-up pencil and all m other worldly possessions into a ver large puddle. To tell the truth, I'v never really got past the gawky stage

Nor had he. He scrabbled about chasing soggy tissues like the ol awkward guy he used to be, trippin over his feet, blushing almost as muc as I was over some of the things w had to recover from the puddle. W almost bumped noses down there, fo a moment, and sprang back as if we'

een stung. Disaster seemed to be part
f it all, whatever it was between us.
'oo much talk perhaps.

"Thanks!" I muttered finally.

"My pleasure!" he croaked, wrink-
ng up that nose that I quite liked,
ickering at me the sharpness of those
lue eyes that I liked very much. I
huffled into the house and he
imbered off down the road.

KERRY, my kid sister, flew
out of the front room
where she'd obviously
been tweaking the
urtains, spying on me as usual.
'ourteen-year-olds can be a real
rag.

"Was that Charlie Wilson who was
issing you in the gutter?" she
reathed, heavily.

"Huh! Chance'd be a fine thing!" I
narled.

"He's fantastic!" she raved, doing
his dreamy look that made her look
ke a rabbit with rigor mortis. "Every-
ne in my class is crazy about him
. . But he's not free! He told Sharon
hat he's suffering from unrequited
love!"

"So that's what's made him such a
pain in the neck, is it?" I snapped. But
I was hurt, really hurt, somehow.
Charlie Wilson wasn't the kind of guy
who falls in love. It didn't go with the
image. I felt he was letting the side
down, and, in some funny way, letting
me down, too.

"Yeah," she continued, as if I'd
never spoken. "With some mysterious girl he once met who had a pet
caterpillar. That's what he told
Sharon, anyway. Dead romantic, isn't
it?"

"Dead . . ." I echoed, choking
back something or other. I was glad
that the doorbell rang to give me
something to do with my very shaky
hands. I shook the door open.

"Er . . ." he said. It wasn't like
him to be lost for words. Charlie
Wilson usually had an answer for
everything, even before you'd thought
of the question.

"Er . . ." I said, but I had an
excuse. Those sharp blue eyes were
staring straight into mine.

"Er — you dropped this. Out of
your bag. Found it down the road," he
fumbled, shoving the crumpled photograph into my hand. It was more
crumpled than ever now. It had
knocked around in my satchel and in
my handbag for two years. It had been
soggy with tears once or twice. Now
it was soggy with rain. It was a very
wet Monday.

But his smile still smiled at me, and
his chains sparkled, and I stood next
to him, in the photograph, with my
eyelash hanging off my cheek. They
used to have this photographer at the
Palais disco in those days. It almost
brought tears to my eyes again . . .

"Coming to the sixth-form disco
tomorrow? With Cuthbert?" he asked
suddenly, with a very shy grin on his
face.

I tried to smile back. He really was
an extraordinarily fantastic guy.

"Sure!" I whispered, shyly.

I WAS A FOOL

I made all sorts of excuses for Paul being seen with Jeannie Lewis—because it was so much easier than facing up to the truth . . .

I COULDN'T believe it when I saw him with Jeannie Lewis, walking across the park, draped round each other as if they'd never been apart. They were too far away for me to catch them up, just to make sure that it really *was* my Paul.

But I knew anyway. I knew every hair of his head, even from the back. I knew the studded denim jacket. I *knew* him . . .

"It was Paul! I know it was!" I sobbed to Kerry. I'd raced round to her house straight away, hoping that she'd be able to give me some explanation. That's what best friends are for, after all, and she'd been my best friend right through the most fantastic love of my life.

She'd listened to every repeated word, each moment of total happiness between the two of us. And she'd listened to what I'd told her about Paul and Jeannie, why it had finished, how awful she'd been to him, how miserable he'd been right through the time they'd been together. And now she listened, again.

"I can't understand it, Tina," she said. "I thought everything was OK between the two of you, even when he didn't turn up on Wednesday . . ."

She'd been at the club with me on Wednesday when I'd waited all evening for Paul. He'd told me he might be late. He even told me where he was going — round to see Jeannie's brother to try to get the records she'd borrowed and never given back. The fact that Paul still went round there hurt, even though I knew that Vic Lewis had always been a friend of his. I'd panicked when he didn't come to the club, but Kerry had calmed me down. She always did.

"He's probably stuck in a conversation with Vic," she'd said. "You know what boys're like once they get talking about football!"

"Yeah! That'll be it!" I sighed, hoping she was right.

I'D TRUSTED HIM

But I'd lost hope when I saw Paul and Jeannie together again. It was what I always dreaded. He'd told me it was over for good, but Jeannie Lewis was twice as pretty as me and twice as clever. I'd never put it past

her to have another try at Paul. I'd trusted him, but not her.

"Maybe — maybe you've got it all wrong, Tina. Maybe . . ." Kerry said.

"Maybe she was just making a play for him? Maybe he was pushing her off?" I asked.

"It's one answer!" she said.

"I reckon I ought to find out what's happening," I sniffed, trying to stop the tears that crawled hopelessly down my cheeks.

Something *was* happening. I was sure of that. Paul had been a bit off-hand with me, even before Wednesday — turning up late for dates, forgetting to tell me he loved me when he kissed me goodnight, always rushing round to see Vic over something or other. I'd told Kerry that it looked to me as if Vic was trying to persuade him to go back to Jeannie, but I knew he wouldn't, ever.

"What're you going to do?" Kerry asked.

"Dunno! Wait for him outside work, I s'pose. I'll ask him to his face!" I decided.

"In front of all his mates?" she asked.

"Why not?" I snapped.

"Well — why not? If you think that's the best way," she said.

I knew that Kerry would think it was a good idea. She'd always known what I had to do next to hang on to Paul. She'd been with me every step of the way, right from the first night when he'd come to sit next to me at the club. She'd been the one who'd told me that I probably had a chance with him. Now, when things looked desperate, she was still there.

I wished she'd been with me the next night, though, when I waited for Paul outside the works' gates. I wished she'd been there to share the fears and the doubts before he came out. I wished she'd been there to say something to help when he saw me, and turned away and walked quickly in the opposite direction.

As it was, the only people to see my tears and to hear my frantic shouting were his work-mates, sniggering past, all jeering at me, elbowing between me and Paul, so that there was no way that I could reach him.

I NEEDED HER ADVICE

"Does that mean it's over, Kerry?" I cried to her over the telephone. "D'you think he's trying to tell me it's over?"

"Looks that way," she said quietly.

"But I wouldn't've thought he'd be like that. I thought he really cared about you . . ."

"He *does*! Shall I give up?" I howled. "Or shall I go round to his house to ask him? I have to know! I have to know whether he's back with Jeannie . . ."

"Be careful," Kerry said.

That's all she said. She knew how much Paul meant to me.

Somehow, though, her encouragement didn't help me as much as I thought it would do. I'd been ready to rush straight round to Paul's house, bang on the door, beg him to explain what was happening, plead with him to talk to me and tell me that he still loved me.

But the urge was ebbing away as I pushed my way out of the telephone box. I started to remember what had just happened, the way I'd yelled to Paul, and he'd turned away while his friends whistled and leered and laughed at me. Remembering made me shiver inside. I had to sit and think.

The club was empty, as it always was early in the evening. Someone was in the corner playing on the Space Invaders machine. A couple of girls were sorting through records. I bought a Coke, and sat in one of the alcoves, trying to remember moments of lost happiness, trying to forget the embarrassment and shame I'd just been through, trying to work out exactly what I was going to say to Paul when I gathered together the courage to knock on his door and ask him, face to face, whether he was still going out with me. I must have sat there for ages, in that alcove, long enough for the club to start filling up, for old friends to drift into other alcoves, for the noisy chatter to begin.

"It's a shame about Tina, isn't it?" I heard Val sigh, somewhere in the dimness. "That Paul's really showing her up now, leaving her flat to go back to Jeannie Lewis!"

"Yeah!" Kerry agreed. "Trouble is, she's not helping at all by chasing after him. If she's not careful she'll show *herself* up."

a reader's true experience

I froze, listening hard. Kerry was supposed to be my best friend! She'd told me what to do, she'd advised me how to behave, she'd given me all the directions for showing myself up . . .

SHE'D NEVER LET ME DOWN

Or had she? I was halfway to my feet, about to storm out of my little corner and tell her what I thought of best friends who turned two-faced — but suddenly stopped. Had she really shown me how to make a fool of myself over Paul? Or had I put the words into her mouth?

Kerry had never let me down, not once. She'd agreed with everything I'd said, agreed that Paul fancied me, agreed that it was all over between him and Jeannie, agreed that she'd never been good for him. She'd just nodded her head when I told her what I wanted to do, because I hadn't given her the chance to say what she really felt. I'd pushed her the way I wanted her to go, and she went because she didn't want to hurt me.

"Trouble is . . ." I heard Kerry continue, "I don't know how to tell her that Paul's been playing her along. How d'you tell someone who's crazy about a boy that he's messing her about? She'd never speak to me again, would she?"

"I know!" Val said. "That's what I mean. Shame, isn't it?"

I'd been crying on and off for days, ever since Paul stood me up that Wednesday night. I'd been crying myself into a belief that I was being beaten by Jeannie Lewis. But it wasn't true. I'd been beaten by my own lies, making myself believe that Paul was mine, and I'd talked Kerry into letting me believe those lies.

She was my best friend. I'd not been fair to either of us. Best friends ought to be able to tell each other the truth, even when it hurts.

I eased myself out of the alcove, and tried to smile as I walked over to where I saw Kerry and Val standing.

"I've made a fool of myself over Paul, haven't I, Kerry?" I asked, as if I'd realised that from the start.

"Never mind!" she grinned. "Nobody noticed!"

She squeezed my hand, but I felt better anyway — relieved that I hadn't found the courage to kick Paul's front door down. It would have been the wrong sort of courage . . .

HIGH NOON!

JANE

DEPUTY DOUG

BUTCH AND DUKE

SUNDIAL

CORPORAL TOM

Do you ever wonder what romance was like, back in the days of cowboys and Indians?

WELL, IT WAS ANYTHING BUT EASY! BY THE WAY, MY NAME IS JANE. THEY CALL ME CALAMITOUS JANE.

Because that's the way things usually turn out for me . . .

BUT I RECKONED I'D BE TAKING YOU TO THE DANCE TOMORROW NIGHT, JANE. YOU AIN'T GOIN' WITH NO-ONE ELSE, ARE YA?

OH, 'COURSE NOT, BUTCH.

EXCEPT FOR DUKE, AND TOM, AND WYATT—THEY ALL WANT TO TAKE ME TO THE DANCE AT OUR LOCAL FORT. FORT NIGHTLY . . .

And right then . . .

SO IT'S TRUE! A TIN-HORN TENDERFOOT IS MESSIN' AROUND WITH MY GAL!

D-DUKE! WHAT ARE YOU DOIN' HERE?

Continued on page 46

43

ARE YOU KIDDING?

Alan was once on "Mastermind," where his specialist subject was "Meat Pies." Do you believe that? If so, don't bother reading this quiz — we can tell you now that your score will be 0! But believe it or not, some of the amazing facts here are absolutely true! So have fun working out which ones!

1. Lena, a foxhound, gave birth to 23 puppies in one go in America in 1944.

2. It's reckoned that Paul McCartney earned £25,000,000 in the year 1979/80.

3. Winston, a trained frog owned by R. Morrison of Stockport, hopped the entire length of London Underground's Bakerloo Line non-stop in three hours, six minutes.

4. Robert Earl Hughes, the heaviest man whose weight has been accurately measured, reached the weight of 76 st. 5 lb. That's even heavier than Alan!

5. The common silkworm produces enough thread in a single day to make a parachute.

6. Mr L. Henry, of Birmingham, ate 736 condensed milk sandwiches in 24 hours in 1979.

7. Susan Montgomery of the U.S.A. blew a bubble gum bubble 19¼ inches in diameter in 1979.

8. In 1977, a French guy called M. Lotito ate a bicycle. A whole bicycle.

9. Anne, of Patches magazine, has arrived at work on time on two separate occasions.

10. The longest title ever to enter the British charts was "Under The Blue Moon We'll Dance Away The Hours Until Our Old Tennessee Home Croons In The Moonlight," released on Stateside Records in 1958, sung by Jeb McGreevy and the Alaskan Foot-Warmers. It made number 23.

11. Robert Foster once stayed underwater for 13 mins. 42½ secs. We mean he stayed underwater *without drowning* for that time!

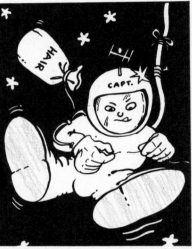

12. If every hair on a *blonde* person's head was laid end to end, they'd stretch to the planet Jupiter and back.

13. The longest kiss in the world was performed in Florida last year and lasted for 5 days 12 hours. This, by the way, beats Kim and Joe's kissing record by 5 days, 11 hours, 59 minutes and 59½ seconds, performed last Christmas.

15. A British firm once exported 1800 tons of sand to Abu Dhabi — which is in the middle of a desert.

16. Mrs Vassilyev of Moscow gave birth to 16 sets of twins! Also 7 sets of triplets. Also 4 sets of quads. That means Mrs Vassilyev had . . . em . . . er . . . 69 little Vassilyevs.

17. The Beane family of Galloway, Scotland, *ate* over 1000 people in the fifteenth century.

19. Bjorn Borg, tennis champion, practises serving with billiard balls to make his arm stronger.

14. The Leaning Tower Of Pisa leans further over by sixteen millimetres per year, and at the present rate, is due to topple over a week on Tuesday.

18. ''Zenyatta Mondatta'' by Police is Britain's fastest-selling album.

20. If you answer all the questions in this quiz correctly, we will send you a cheque for two million pounds.

HOW DID YOU DO?

1. Yes, it's true. Hard luck for any fox in that neighbourhood!

2. True as well — even more than The Ed. earns!

3. False. It's lies from start to finish!

4. True. Although Alan's determined to beat it.

5. Nonsense. It'd have to be about the size of an elephant!

6. Utter drivel. Well, as far as we know . . .

7. True. Almost as big as The Ed.'s head!

8. He did, you know. What a weird guy. Maybe he was up with snails.

9. This is a falsie. She's only been on time once, when her alarm clock was an hour and a half fast, and she arrived four minutes early.

10. False, but it's a great idea for a song, innit?

11. Yes, he really did. Don't try it, though — you'd probably beat the world drowning record.

12. False — unless your hair's hundreds of miles long!

13. Yep, that's how long it lasted. And *without* super-glue!

14. False. Actually, it's only one millimetre per year — but it could fall at any time, according to some architects.

15. Yes, they did. They needed special-size grains for filtering water, apparently.

16. Trueski. Cor, think of the laundry bills . . .

17. Mactrue. They really did. Yeuch!

18. Sorry, Police fans, but it's false. Correct answer — The Beatles' ''White Album.''

19. False. And unless he wants to practise arm-breaking, he never will.

20. We're not telling you the answer to this one. Sneaky, eh?!

1-7 Your guesses didn't really pay off, did they? Some people will believe anything!

8-15 You've obviously got a nose for a leg-pull. Although we thought all of them sounded ridiculous!

16-20 No-one's ever going to catch you out, are they? That's because you're either a real clever clogs — or you cheated!

But next moment . . .

IT'S TOO LATE, DEPUTY! BUTCH AN' DUKE HAVE ALREADY FACED EACH OTHER IN THE MIDDLE OF THE STREET . . .

OH NO! WHAT HAPPENED?

WELL, THEM BOYS TOOK SO LONG DECIDIN' WHO SHOULD DRAW FIRST, THAT THE STAGECOACH COME ALONG AND KNOCKED 'EM BOTH DOWN! I NEVER SEE'D SUCH A SIGHT!

I'VE HEARD OF BEING STAGE-STRUCK, BUT THAT'S RIDICULOUS! ARE THEY HURT?

NOPE, JUST A MITE RUN-DOWN. THEY DIDN'T EVEN GET THE CHANCE TO DRAW THEIR GUNS.

AH! A NO-SCORE DRAW . . .

So we hurried round to old Doc Boone's place . . .

DUKE! BUTCH! ARE YOU ALL RIGHT?

SURE, HONEY. BUT WE STILL AIN'T DECIDED WHO'S TAKIN' YOU TO THE DANCE TOMORROW.

THAT DON'T MATTER NOW. I'M ARRESTIN' YOU BOTH FOR DISTURBIN' THE PEACE. THAT MEANS TWO DAYS IN JAIL . . .

WHAT? BUT IT WAS THE STAGE THAT DISTURBED THE PEACE!

But he marched them off to jail anyway . . .

DANG-BLAST IT! WITH DUKE AND BUTCH BOTH IN JAIL, WHO'S GONNA TAKE ME TO THE DANCE NOW?

WAIT A MINUTE! OF COURSE! THERE'S CORPORAL TOM AT THE FORT. WE'VE BEEN OUT TOGETHER. HE'LL TAKE ME TO THE DANCE!

I rode out to Fort Nightly, but . . .

I CAN'T TAKE YOU TO THE DANCE, JANE. I GOT EXTRA DUTIES TO DO . . .

SOMEONE SENT THE CAPTAIN A TELEGRAM, SAYIN' I'D SNEAKED OFF THE POST TO DATE YOU. IT WAS SIGNED 'THE STRANGE LONER!'

I WISH I KNEW WHO THIS STRANGE LONER GUY WAS, HE SEEMS DETERMINED TO SPOIL THINGS FOR ME.

SO, AS CORPORAL PUNISHMENT, I'VE GOT TO DO EXTRA DUTIES ALL WEEK!

I headed back to town . . .

I asked Deputy Doug next day . . .

I-I DON'T KNOW, JANE. THERE'S NO-ONE OF THAT NAME IN TOWN . . .

I WANT YOU TO DO SOMETHING ABOUT IT! YOU'RE THE LAW—YOU DIDN'T WIN THAT BADGE ON SEARCH FOR A STAR, DID YOU?

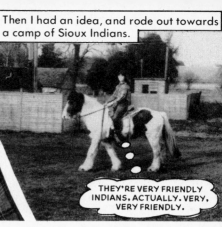

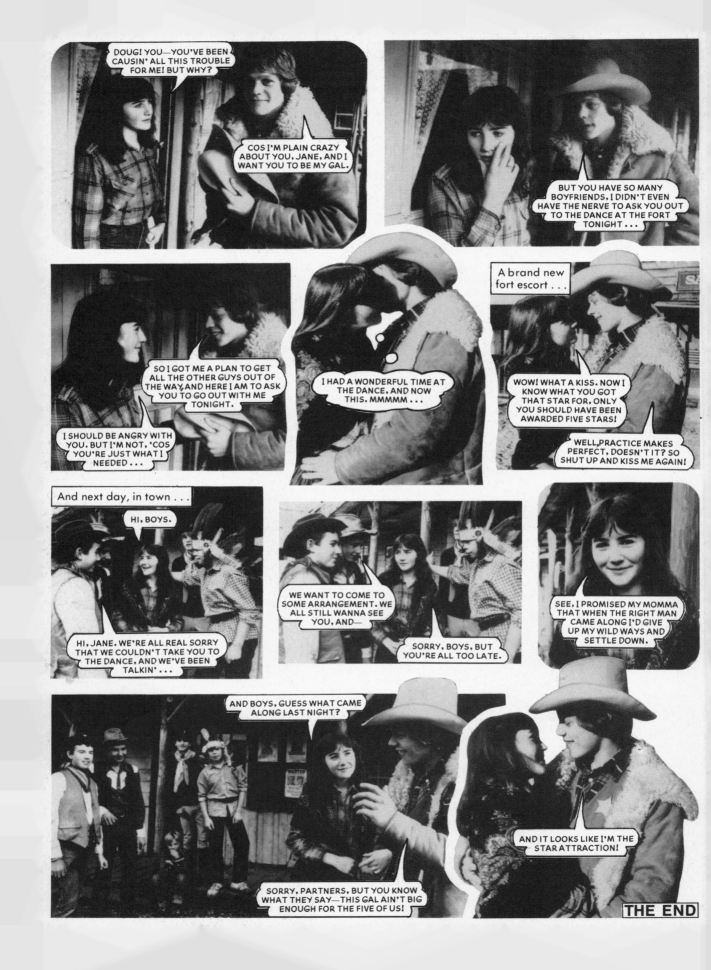

EAT TO THE BEAT!

Honey-cakes for Sting? Something nutty for Madness? What would you give your favourite pop stars if they just happened to drop by for dinner? Whip up a couple of these delicious dishes and even if you don't have pop stars round your house in droves, at least you'll have found a lovely, tasty way to fill the long, cold, winter evenings!

CHEW A CHOWDER WITH CLIFF PILCHARD . . .

1 packet tomato and vegetable soup
1½ pints water
2 oz. tiny shell pasta or noodles
1 clove garlic, crushed
1 green pepper, finely chopped
1 medium can salmon

1. Flake the salmon, removing bones if desired.
2. Make up the soup with 1½ pints of water (or as directed on packet) and bring to boil.
3. Add the pasta and crushed garlic and simmer gently until pasta is tender.
4. Add the finely-chopped green pepper and flaked salmon, then heat together.
5. Serve hot with crusty bread.

TRY A TRUFFLE FOR HOT CHOCOLATE . . .

1 lb. cake crumbs
8 oz. sifted icing sugar
4 oz. cocoa powder
¼ pint milk
3 oz. chocolate vermicelli
18 paper cake cases

1. Mix the cake crumbs with the icing sugar and cocoa powder.
2. Bind them together with the milk to make a fairly stiff mixture.
3. Divide it into 18 even-sized pieces and roll each one into a ball.
4. Sprinkle the chocolate vermicelli on to a plate, then roll each ball in them until evenly coated.
5. Place the Chocolate Truffles in paper cases before serving.

WHAT ABOUT A PIZZA FOR THE POLIZZA?

For the dough:
8 oz. self-raising flour
1 teaspoonful baking powder
1 medium egg
½ teaspoonful salt
1½ oz. margarine
¼ pint (less 2 tablespoonfuls) milk
For the sauce:
1 tablespoonful oil
½ clove garlic, finely chopped
Salt and pepper
1 small can anchovy fillets
½ medium onion, finely chopped
2 tablespoonfuls tomato purée
1½ oz. finely-grated cheese
1 small jar, stuffed olives

1. Sift dry dough ingredients into bowl and rub in fat to fine breadcrumbs consistency.
2. Mix to a soft dough with lightly-beaten egg and milk and knead lightly until smooth.
3. Heat oil, add onion and garlic and cook slowly till soft but not brown.
4. Stir in tomato purée and seasonings and remove from heat.
5. Turn the dough on to a lightly-floured board and roll out to ½-¾ of an inch thick.
6. Cut into 8 rounds with a 3-inch cutter.
7. Place the rounds on a greased and floured baking tray, allowing room between each for spreading.
8. Make a "well" in each round with the floured base of a jam jar or tumbler about 2½ inches across.
9. Fill each "well" with the tomato sauce and cover with grated cheese.
10. Top with anchovy fillets and halved, stuffed olives.
11. Bake near the top of a hot oven (425 deg. F., Gas Mark 7) for about 20 minutes and serve at once.

ATTRACT ANTS WITH CREAMY CAULIFLOWER . . .

1 small cauliflower
½ oz. butter
½ oz. flour
½ pint milk
Salt and pepper
½ a small onion, finely grated
2 thick slices ham, diced
2 tablespoonfuls cream
1 tablespoonful mayonnaise

1. Trim outer leaves from the cauliflower. Boil, whole, in salted water until tender.
2. Meanwhile, to make the sauce, melt the butter in a pan, sprinkle in the flour and gradually add the milk, stirring all the time.
3. Season with salt and pepper and add onion.
4. Blend in the diced ham, cream and mayonnaise.
5. Reheat very gently, *without allowing to boil.*
6. Drain the cauliflower well.
7. Arrange on a dish and cover with the ham sauce.
8. Serve with potatoes or boiled rice.

Sheba was the most beautiful dog I'd ever seen — and Jem had given her to me. And at first I was too happy to bother about where he'd got her...

A GIRL'S BEST FRIEND...

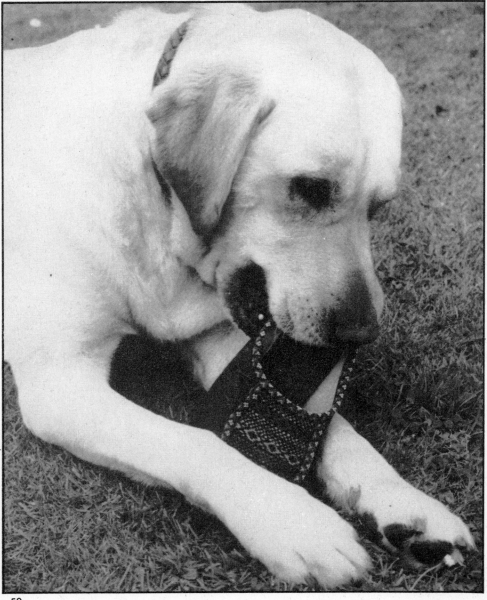

I THOUGHT I'd got used to Jem's craziness, but that beat it all, the morning of my birthday, when I opened the door to see him standing there, wonky grin and all, holding that lead. And attached to the lead was the most beautiful, floppy-eared, brown-eyed golden Labrador I'd ever seen, as beautiful a dog as Pronto, my old Great Dane, who'd died of old age a month before.

"Happy birthday!" Jem laughed. "Shake hands with your present! Sheba, shake!"

And the dog lifted one heavy paw, holding it up for me to take.

I just stood there, holding on to this silky paw, tears in my eyes, not knowing what to say or do next, bowled over by it all. Mum and Dad had promised me another dog, but I'd wanted to take my time choosing. I knew what I wanted. And Sheba was exactly what I wanted . . .

"But — how on earth did you manage to afford her, or train her or . . . ?" I spluttered at last.

"Ask no questions!" Jem told me, tapping the side of his nose with his finger. So I didn't. I should have done, though. I shouldn't have waited until all the doubts started crashing in on me.

Jem was always doing strange things. I'd refused to go out with him for ages. Most of my friends said he was odd, and no-one knew much about him, except that he was a student at the local college, in digs, and went home almost every weekend to some back of beyond place in the country. But he kept asking me for a date every time I went into the corner shop where he helped out in the evenings, and in the end, I had to give way.

HIS EYES WERE SO STRANGE

"He's a loony!" Debbie kept telling me. "Can't you tell by his eyes?"

I'd look into his deep green twinkling eyes, and wonder whether they were mad eyes. They were strange eyes, misty with secrets, suddenly alight with mischief, but not mad eyes.

I liked his eyes, I decided, that first time I went out with him. And I liked his joking, his laughter, the way he made me feel. But I wondered why he told me so little about himself, and why he clammed up every time I asked him too many questions.

Mum liked him. Dad wasn't sure. "Be careful, Julie!" he told me. "There's something funny about that boy. What d'you know about him?" And I'd have to admit I knew almost nothing, except that he was studying Surveying, and that there was a sadness in him that I hadn't quite put my finger on.

And the only time I saw him really almost give way, was the night I told him about Pronto, about how much I missed the friendship and companionship of that huge soft dog, the way he'd come to me each evening when I came home from school and place his silky head in my lap, as if he'd been waiting for me all day. I knew how old and tired and sick he was, but he was always there, waiting, welcoming, as if I was important to him. He'd helped me through all the really bad times when I felt awkward and bitter and different. The really bad times after Mum and Dad finally found the courage to tell me that I wasn't their daughter at all — that I'd been adopted.

I told Jem all this. Everything. I don't know why. Maybe I was reaching out to him, trying to explain my own sadness in the hope that he'd tell

me about his. But all he did was hold my hand, and stroke my cheek, and settle my head into the warm curve of his shoulder.

"I'll get you a dog, Julie, one day!" he promised. "Everyone ought to have a dog!" and his voice was huskier than usual . . .

I didn't even take him seriously. I should have done.

After a month or so of going steady with him I'd learnt all about his funny surprise presents, and the way he never let me down or forgot anything I told him. Debbie would probably have said that proved he was a loony. Most of the boys we knew pretended that girls didn't matter. I knew I mattered to Jem. Especially when he brought me Sheba . . .

Mum just said, "Oh!" when we walked into the house, all three of us. She looked as stunned as I'd been. But I had to laugh when Jem made Sheba repeat the hand-shaking act, and Mum just had to sit down in amazement.

It was the best birthday I'd ever had. Jem and I took Sheba

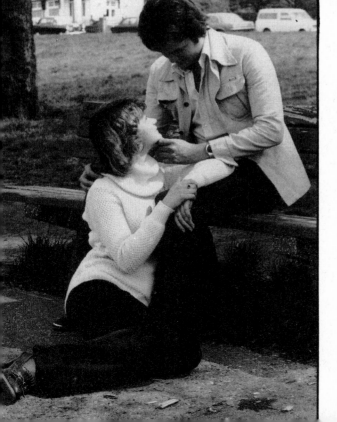

down on the common and he showed me everything she could do. Some of her tricks surprised even me — the way she'd sit and wait at the kerb until the road was absolutely clear, the way she'd walk at heel even without a lead, and not be distracted by any other dog. She was a dog in a million, and she took to me straight away, bringing sticks to me, and not Jem.

"Why?" I asked Jem, as we walked home. "Why did you spend all that money on a real pedigree dog like that, just for me?"

"It's a long story. I didn't buy her. Just be satisfied with that for the moment!" he told me. "Don't you know how much you mean to me, Julie?" and then his arm curled round me and clutched me to him.

No boy had ever looked at me the way he did, or cared for me the way he did, or made me feel so soft and gentle inside, the way he did. He wasn't mad. He was just a bit out of the ordinary, this tall boy with the strange green eyes, and too much love in him. I knew I'd fallen for him and his kindness in a way I found difficult to understand.

HE SAID SHE WAS STOLEN

And then Dad started on me. I think Sheba worried him. Sheba, you see, wouldn't have much to do with Dad. She was my dog, or Mum's, and we were both too happy with her to do much thinking about where she came from. But Dad did. He started off with niggling doubts about her lead and name-tag being old, and about the way she'd been trained.

"That dog's been someone's pet!" he kept saying. "Did he say he'd got her from a dogs' home? Have you checked with the police to see if a dog like that's been reported missing? I don't trust that boy of yours. There's something very funny about him, Julie!"

He kept going on and on. In the end, the doubts got the better of me, too. Jem said he hadn't bought the dog, but no-one would have put a dog like that into a home, or given it away. She was too valuable. And she was so loving, at least to me and Mum. Someone must have cared for her a great deal to make her so gentle.

"She's stolen!" Dad said firmly. "I'm convinced of it! That boy's capable of anything. The way he runs about after you, Julie, I'd not put it past him to steal that dog just to make you happy. I'm not saying he's not done you a lot of good. You've certainly cheered up a bit since you knew him. But I think he's got a screw loose or something. He looks a bit funny at times!"

"Oh no!" Mum said.

"Oh no!" I said. But I knew Debbie'd agree, and even I wasn't all that sure about Jem.

And then Mum finally clinched it. She handed me the paper one day, the local paper, with one of the adverts underlined.

"Lost," it said. "Labrador, answering to the name of Sheba. Please telephone 23486. Reward offered. Children pining."

A little dark shiver rippled down my spine. Mum looked hard at me.

"Well?" she asked.

And then Jem knocked at the door, grinning as usual, his strange eyes twinkling as usual. "Let's take Sheba for a walk!" he said.

I tried to put him off. I really wanted to talk to Mum, but Sheba was standing, wagging her tail, and I couldn't resist going out with her, one last time. I collected her lead, trying to hold back the tears of disappointment, imagining Debbie telling me, "I told you, didn't I?" and hearing Dad's words again — "That boy's capable of anything!"

HE TOLD ME THE TRUTH

I knew that this was the last time we'd be together, the three of us, or even the two of us. I had to get the truth out of Jem. I had to finish with him.

"You ring and tell those children we'll bring her round later!" I whispered to Mum before I left. She looked as hurt as I was, but I knew she'd do it. It was only right.

Then we walked along to the common as usual, Jem and I holding hands, as usual. Sheba walking at heel, as usual. But it wasn't as usual inside me. I kept glancing at Jem, at the frown that wrinkled his forehead, and always had done, at the cloudiness in his green eyes, at the tenderness

Continued on page 56.

1. Here are the stars of the successful "Not The Nine O'Clock News." Can you name them?

2. Who is he and whose backing band does he play in?

3. What Broadway play is David Bowie starring in here?

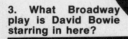

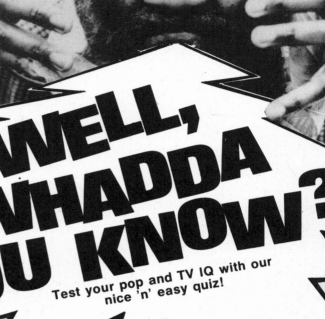

WELL, WHADDA YOU KNOW?

Test your pop and TV IQ with our nice 'n' easy quiz!

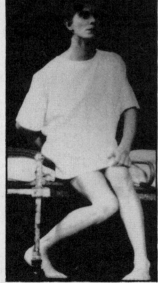

4. What film does this scene come from? Name the two stars.

5. This is the lead singer of a group which made a comeback after six years. Who is he? What's the group? What single took them to the top again?

6. What programme does Brian Trueman present?

7. Name these comedians.

B

C

D

E

8. The original line-up of Dexy's Midnight Runners arrive at Euston Station, but who are they searching for?

9. Who are these two Muppet characters?

10. Name this line-up from "Get It Together."

11. Here are two famous crook catchers. Can you name the TV programme they appeared in, the characters they played and their real names?

A   B

12. He had a No. 1 hit with an Italian flavour. Who is he and what was the record?

13. He's a bit older now and stars in a children's programme — who is he?

14. Who ARE these people?

A   B   C   D   E

15. Last, but not least, who's the hunk at the top of the first page?!

ANSWERS

1 Mel Smith, Rowan Atkinson, Pamela Stephenson and Griff Rhys Jones. 2 Wilko Johnson — he plays with Ian Dury's Blockheads. 3 The Elephant Man. 4 The film was "Breaking Glass" and the stars were Hazel O'Connor and Phil Daniels. 5 He's Noddy Holder from Slade and the hit record was, "We'll Bring The House Down." 6 Screen Test. 7a — Les Dawson, b — Cannon and Ball, c — Jim Davidson, d — Kelly Monteith, e — Benny Hill. 8 The young soul rebels. 9 Waldorf and Statler. 10 Mega Nicol, Ollie Beak and Roy North. 11a "Juliet Bravo" with Stephanie Turner playing Inspector Jean Darblay, b — "Shoestring" with Trevor Eve playing Eddie Shoestring. 12 Joe Dolce and the record was "Shaddupa Your Face." 13 He's Todd Carty from "Grange Hill" making his stage debut at 13. 14a — Suggs of Madness, b — Joe Strummer of The Clash, c — Mike Oldfield, d — Kate Bush, e — Steve Strange of Visage. 15 Lenny Henry from "Tiswas."

Did you get them all right? Of course you did! That's because you read Patches every week, isn't it?

HELP!
I NEED SOMEBODY...

Patches gets hundreds of problem letters every week dealing with just about every subject you could think of. But since this is our Annual, we thought we'd pick out some of the "most-asked" questions in the hope that we can help as many readers as possible! If you don't find the answer to your problem here, though, don't despair. You can always write to us at, "Help," Patches, 20 Cathcart Street, Kentish Town, London NW5 3BN. (Remember to enclose a stamped, addressed envelope if you want a personal reply).

Remember, now, there's no need for you to sit about worrying all on your own — share your problems with us. We can't promise to solve everything, but we're good listeners and maybe our advice will help you solve them yourself. So what're you waiting for? Get writing!

OH, BROTHER

You seem to be able to solve most people's problems, can you solve mine? It's my brother! He's a real pain in the neck — he's always picking fights and hitting me for no reason and if I retaliate, he goes crying to Mum or Dad and I get a row! It's just not fair because he starts a lot more fights than me. I'm really beginning to hate him now but I don't see what I can do about it. Help me before I go mad! I'm 14 and he's 10.

I wish I could invent a magical anti-brother potion — I'd make a fortune! Unfortunately, that's not on, though, so it looks like you're stuck with him. So what you must do now is try to make the best of a bad job. Look at it this way: he's going to be around for a long time yet so you might as well aim to make life as peaceful as possible!

First off, don't play him at his own game. If you hit back you'll lose, right? And he'll have the satisfaction of seeing you suffer. But if you try to pretend he doesn't bother you, he'll be flummoxed. So don't rise to his bait and don't argue back — just agree with him! Don't hit him back — just smile and get quietly out of the way. Yes, I know it'll be very difficult sometimes, but if you can manage to keep your temper long enough to get up to your room you can always work the frustration off by bashing your teddy!

Try to discuss your brother calmly with your mum. For example, "I don't know how you put up with him, Mum, I can hardly control my temper sometimes . . ." I've a feeling your mum must be almost as fed up as you so I'll bet she'll relish the chance of finding an ally!

P.S. I know this may sound incredible now, but one day in the future, you'll probably grow quite fond of your brother!

LEFT OUT

I'm so lonely and miserable I just don't know if life's worth bothering about any more. You see, my best friend and I have fallen out. We'd been friends since we were four and we were really close. We used to share everything and tell each other all our secrets. But then this other girl, Mary, came to our school and started to hang around with us. At first that didn't bother me much and in a way it was nice to have someone else about, but gradually they started to meet each other without me and they used to talk about all the things they'd done and all the fun they had and it made me feel really left out. Eventually, Kath and I had a big row over it and now they're not speaking to me at all.

All the other girls have their own friends, so I'm on my own nearly all the time. I'm beginning to hate school because of this and I used to quite like it, too. What can I do?

It's not a nice experience, losing a close friend this way, but in a way it was inevitable, you know. You couldn't really have expected to keep Kath all to yourself ALL the time, could you? Actually, it wasn't really a good idea to be so dependant on her anyway. It's good to have a special friend but you'd have been better to have had a few other pals, too.

I'm sure they didn't deliberately exclude you or mean to hurt you by discussing what they did together. If you'd given them a chance, I'm sure they'd have made that clear! So now I have two pieces of advice for you. One — go and apologise to Mary and Kath. Yes, I know they were partly to blame but so were you! Besides, it won't hurt to say sorry, will it? And it'll be good to be back on speaking terms with them.

The second piece of advice is to spread yourself about a bit more! Be prepared to share Kath with Mary and try to make some other friends, too. Join a school club or local youth organisation and you'll soon get to know other girls (and boys!). Once you've done that you needn't be lonely again!

I'M SO SHY

I'd dearly love to have a boyfriend but I'm terribly shy. Every time I meet a boy I turn bright red and stammer like an idiot, so they soon get fed up and wander away. I've even tried practising conversations at home, but when it's the real thing I always dry up and make a fool of myself. I'm getting really depressed because all my friends seem to find it so easy to talk to boys and they're all getting boyfriends now so soon I'll be all on my own. Please help.

We get loads of letters like this from boys as well as girls, so take heart — you're not alone! This is the sort of problem for which there's only one real cure — time. As you get older and more experienced you will find it easier to relate to boys, so it's really just a question of trying to help time along.

Remember that many of the boys you meet will be every bit as scared as you — more so, in fact, because they're often expected to make the first moves. *Don't* think you have to put on airs and graces or make scintillating conversation all the time. "He" wants to get to know the *real* you, so just try to be natural — some boys actually prefer quiet girls, you know. If you're stuck for words, ask him about himself — his hobbies, favourite subjects, tastes in music, TV and so on. Then all you have to do is listen and look fascinated! Once the ice is broken I think you'll find it a lot easier than you'd

imagined to get on friendly terms with boys, and once that's happened, romance will follow quite naturally!

WEIGH IN

I'm 14, 5 ft. 3 in. tall and I weigh 8½ stones. I think I'm too fat but my mum won't let me go on a diet — she says it's dangerous at my age. But I hate wearing tight jeans 'cos they make my thighs look enormous! Can you tell me a safe way to lose weight, please, and tell me what I should weigh?

In a way, your mum's right, you shouldn't go on a strict diet because you're still developing and need extra proteins, etc., to ensure that you grow healthily. But if you feel you're a bit too heavy, it certainly won't do you any harm to lose a little weight. I can't tell without seeing you what your ideal weight should be — that depends on your build. The best guide is to look at yourself, without any clothes on, in a mirror. If any bits of you are *flabby,* then you're probably overweight.

The simple rule to remember is — eat LESS and do MORE. Eat your three well-balanced meals a day, avoiding greasy foods and including plenty of fresh fruit and veg. Don't nibble between meals and if you must have a snack, choose an apple or something instead of a chocolate bar!

Increase the amount of exercise you get in as many ways as possible. Walk instead of bussing, jog instead of walking, do 15 minutes toe-touching and running on the spot every morning and night. Take up cycling or swimming or badminton, and disco dance like mad! Do anything and everything you enjoy, in fact, because the more the better, because exercising burns off calories and it's calories — or rather a *surplus* of calories — which make you fat. Good luck!

I COULDN'T BEAR TO LOSE HIM

I've been going out with Don for nearly a year. We were really close, always laughing together and hardly ever fighting. But just recently he's begun to change. You see, he's started a new job and all he seems to want to do is talk about it. He goes on and on about how great everyone is and he never wants to hear about MY life anymore. Also, he's been seeing less of me because he wants to go out with his mates from work instead. I wouldn't mind so much but there're girls, too, and I'm sure he must fancy one of them. He says he doesn't, but why else would he have started to go off me? Please help — I couldn't bear to lose him.

I know you don't want even to think of losing Don, but I'm afraid that sooner or later you're going to have to face up to the fact that he's drifting away from you. That's a terribly painful thing to have to bear but there's really nothing you can do about it now. Obviously, he's excited by the new world which is opening up before him and I'm sure you don't want to hold him back. Besides, he'd resent you bitterly if you tried, so don't be tempted to chase after him or beg him to stay with you. Let him go, OK? I'm sure you know, deep down, that it's the only thing you can do.

Of course, you'll be very upset, so go right ahead and have a few long weeping sessions — tears are marvellous therapy for a broken heart! But once they've stopped, make a big effort to put all this in the past. You have your own future to consider from now on so pick up the pieces and get yourself involved in life again. If you keep busy, you *will* get over Don eventually — I promise!

PARENT TROUBLE. . .

My parents are really getting me down. They don't let me go out at all during the week and if I get to any discos on Saturday, Dad always comes to pick me up at 9.30! All my friends can stay till it finishes at 11 o'clock and they get to go out on weekdays as well. I've tried to talk to my parents and to tell them I'd be able to look after myself, but they won't listen. The worst thing is, there's this boy I fancy and I'm pretty sure he's going to ask me out soon. If he does, I'd have to say no because my folks would go mad at the very thought of me dating a boy! How can I persuade them to trust me?

It's not simply a question of persuading them, you're going to have to prove that you're mature enough to look after yourself! I know it seems terribly unfair that you should be treated this way but you must realise that making a big fuss isn't going to help at all. If you shout and moan about it you'll only make yourself look childish and that's the last thing you need! Unfortunately, winning their trust will be a fairly slow process but it will be worth it in the long run, so be patient, OK?

Begin by getting into their good books — be extra helpful around the house. Do all your chores plus a few extra. Make them unasked-for cuppas and be nice and polite all the time. Then, once they're in a good mood, tactfully ask them if you can stay a bit later at the disco. Let your dad come to get you as usual, but at 10.30 instead. Don't push your luck, though, leave the weekday outings and dating issues till later. One step at a time!

If you see this boy at the disco you can spend some time with him there, but if he does ask you to meet him elsewhere, just tell him the truth. If he really likes you, he won't mind waiting, you'll see.

Continued from page 51.

in his glance when he smiled at me, and it all seemed strange and wrong suddenly, that the boy I'd fallen in love with could be someone I didn't know at all, not really . . .

"You stole her, didn't you?" I asked him quietly, trying not to cry, as he let Sheba off the lead in the common.

"Yes, I stole her," he said, matter-of-factly, as if it wasn't something to be ashamed of at all. But I was glad he'd told the truth now, at last. If my heart was going to be broken, I wanted it broken by truth.

He must have realised that. He didn't even try to touch me or hold me. I wondered if he'd seen the advertisement, too, and knew, as I did, that it was all over — the love and the lying, the laughter and the secrets.

"I stole her from my grandfather," he added. And then, and only then, while Sheba worried a stick some distance away, he turned to me, and took my arm. My eyes were filled with tears of relief, bewilderment, questions. His were filled with sadness.

"I'm a bit like you, Julie," he said. "My grandparents brought me up after my mum and dad died. But they were pretty old, and my grandma was very ill. She died, earlier

this year. I keep going back to the farm to see my grandfather, but he's very bad now, tired and ill, and bad-tempered.

"Sheba was Grandma's dog. She couldn't see very well, and Sheba was devoted to her. They relied on each other. But Grandad hated the dog after Grandma died. I had to see she had a good home. I couldn't have her in my digs. Maybe I should have told you, but I didn't want to explain everything. It all hurts too much. It brings it all back, you see . . ."

I swallowed. I knew about hurting. I remembered the hate and the hurt I'd felt those months ago when I'd found out I was adopted, wondering why I hadn't been loved by my real mum and dad like other babies. And I remembered the hate I'd felt for Mum and Dad for not telling me, and the comfort I'd found in Pronto, until he died.

It must have been the same sort of hurt that Jem felt, the same loneliness. He only had his old grandad, miles away, and this dog. Nothing else, except me. All that love in him, bottled up in sadness, had found me, as I'd found him. Some people call that "strangeness." But it's loneliness, that's all. And I hated myself for ever doubting, and not realising that.

I flung my arms round his neck and nuzzled my wet cheek against his. Sheba padded up to sit panting at our feet.

"I think I love you, Jem!" I whispered, as he kissed me. What I wanted to tell him was that I'd started trusting him at last. But love and trust are almost the same thing.

And then we strolled home together, wound in each other's arms, Sheba trotting beside us, talking quietly about things we both understood, sad things that we could share now, and turn into happiness, back home to Mum.

She was smiling, too, beckoning me into the kitchen where she whispered in my ear. *"Their* Sheba was a *black* Labrador!"

"I'll explain everything later!" I whispered back at her.

But I didn't really need to. She could probably tell that everything had sorted itself out. She only had to look at me, and at Jem, and at the laughter in his green eyes . . .

Friends..

EVERYBODY needs friends, although not necessarily to the same degree. An outgoing girl might start to feel lonely as soon as she says goodbye to a bunch of friends, but a loner can spend a lot of time on her own without noticing she is alone because she doesn't need company quite so much.

But if you didn't have pals, mates and best friends, the world would be a much less colourful place, wouldn't it? Well, who would you brag to/commiserate with over this year's exam results? Who'd listen to your endless chatter about the gorgeous guy who delivers the papers?

You may be really close to your family, but you do need friends – people who aren't related to you, because you'll learn different approaches to life from them, you'll come across different ideas which will help you form your own opinions, your own ideas, and help you broaden your outlook.

It's great to have friends, and if it all comes quite naturally to you, you'll know what it means. BUT, if you've ever had problems with friends, ever hit a bad patch with a best friend, or felt suddenly lonely and out of step with the rest of the crowd, then this is for you.

CAN'T MAKE FRIENDS?

WHILE you're growing up, there are lots of upheavals to cope with. Perhaps a new school, new options to choose, college, or maybe a job — and changes like this tend to affect your social life, too. Sometimes you simply lose touch with the friends you have and find it hard to make new ones.

Finding new friends often means you've got to be a bit pushy. You've got to let people know you're around. Think of someone you know who's popular and we bet she's probably natural, easy to approach and full of enthusiasm, but she won't try *too* hard, either. We've all met the kind of person who's got a desperate glint in her eye and who bears down on you with all the subtlety of a leech — and let's face it, in this situation it's only human nature to want to back off!

If you want to make friends, by all means be direct, even a bit pushy, but do allow the other person a bit of room for manoeuvre — allow her some space to reach out to you, so that it's not all one-sided. There is a right and a wrong way to go about getting to know someone better. Take, for instance, a girl we'll call Sally who goes to a comprehensive in her third year. Anna shares a lot of her classes and looks nice, but how does Sally get to know her? There's a choice of two basic approaches . . .

APPROACH No 1.
Sally: Are you doing anything tomorrow night, Anna?
Anna: Er, no . . .
Sally: Oh good. You can come to my house. I've got a new L.P. I've done my room up specially

and Mum's going to lay on a special supper.

APPROACH No 2.
Sally: Hi, Anna! If you're not doing anything tomorrow night, come along to my house. Lisa and Joan are coming. We're going to swap records and I'm hoping you can all fill me in on the school gossip.
Anna: Yeah — Great! What time?

No prizes for guessing the right approach in that situation. In the second approach, Sally sounded much more casual. She didn't make too much fuss about it all, and let Anna know she'd invited two other girls — so conversation would be that much easier. And she also let Anna know in a discreet way that she felt pretty new and green but was eager to be one of them.

Who Needs 'Em?

Everyone, that's who! But making friends – and being a good friend yourself – isn't always easy, so, to give you a helping hand, we present the Patches Good Friend Guide!

SHRINKING VIOLETS APPLY HERE

WHAT if you can't bring yourself to make a direct approach in case you're snubbed? What if the very thought of making the first move makes you blush, stammer and break out in a cold sweat?

When you're shy, it's easy to wait for other people to make the first move and then blame them when they don't, and in the same way, if you're a newcomer, it's easy to convince yourself that everyone knows everyone else, that they've formed their clique and don't need anyone else. But there's always room for a new face!

There's probably someone who looks more approachable than the others in this kind of situation. Talk to her and, if you can, admit to your shyness. There's nothing more appealing than some-

one who admits to a weakness — it gives the other person a chance to help! Don't wait too long before you make that first approach, though, because it's awfully easy to tell yourself tomorrow, next week, next month it'll all be different, and meantime you've been labelled a loner, someone who's happier left alone.

If you're shy, it can be easier to make friends through sports clubs, hobby groups or classes. Check after-school activities and community centres, and get a list of what's going on from your local library. It can be easier to make friends while you're trying to untangle your limbs from a double knot during a yoga session, or giggling over a lop-sided pot you've thrown at pottery classes!

BREAKING UP

SUPPOSING making friends isn't your problem, but keeping them certainly is. Friendships often break up because of outside influences, but what if your friends simply keep dropping you and it happens not once or twice but again and again?

Try to find out why — and be ruthlessly honest with yourself. Why did she go off

with someone else? Was it honestly always her fault?

It's a fact of life that as you mature you can simply grow away from friends you've known for ages, and the friendships are discarded like last summer's sandals, but if all your friendships die before they've had a chance to develop, check our list, and see if you've been guilty of some of these . . .

. . . SEVEN DEADLY SINS!

1. Gossip about everything she's told you in confidence 'cos it's simply too juicy to keep to yourself . . .
2. Look on her as your number-one rival in terms of looks, clothes, the amount of pocket money you get, and feel envious and jealous of any successes she has . . .
3. Use her. Call her up only when you're really at a loose end and then cancel everything when *he* phones and asks to take you out . . .
4. Monopolise the conversation. After all, your news is much more fascinating than hers. Immediately look terribly bored whenever she opens her mouth . . .
5. Use her as a stooge when boys are around. Tease her, make her blush and let the boys see what a razor sharp wit you have . . .
6. Make a huge scene if she wants to go swimming with Karen. It doesn't matter that you hate swimming and never go — she's your friend, isn't

she? End this scene in a dramatic "her" or "me" choice . . .
7. Do be sure you get your own way, at least 99% of the time . . .

Ouch! Well, you wouldn't be human if one or more of these seven deadly sins didn't make you wince a bit!

SO WHO'S PERFECT?

NO-ONE, thank goodness. Who can think of anything more nauseating than a "best" friend who oozes self-righteousness, kindness and generosity . . . who turns the other cheek and makes you feel guilty all the time?

The best kind of friend to have is someone who's human, just like you . . . someone who knows what it's like to go through agonies because of a spot, or a cold sore . . . someone who gets ratty when you've been moody and niggly all day — and shouts back at you when you shout at her. She's also someone who makes demands — on your time, your

loyalty, your patience. That way you're much more liable to have a fifty-fifty relationship — you'll learn to give and take, and *not* be the pig-headed, self-centred selfish person we all are basically when we can get away with it!

The more value you place on a friendship, and the more you learn to look on it as something precious — the more special it will be.

Friendships have their ups and downs. Some you win and some you lose. One thing's for sure, though, you've got the whole of your life in front of you and you'll be making new friends all the time!

SHE'S MY GIRL

BEING WITH ROSANNA IS THE BEST THING THAT EVER HAPPENED TO ME. ALL THE GUYS HERE WISH THEY WERE ME.

And who could blame them? She had the same effect on me the first time I saw her.

...I SAID, DO I SIGN HERE?

UH—SORRY, YES...

WOW! SHE'S GORGEOUS!

She really knocked me for six...

MISS CLARK—WAIT— I FORGOT TO GIVE YOU YOUR DAD'S COVER NOTE...

I don't know where I got the courage from...

W- WOULD YOU LIKE TO ...EM...HOW ABOUT COMING TO THE PICTURES WITH ME SOME NIGHT?

WELL, I—ALL RIGHT, THAT'D BE NICE. HOW ABOUT TOMORROW NIGHT?

I couldn't believe it...

SHE'S SO BEAUTIFUL— AND SHE'S WITH ME!

ENJOYING THE FILM?

OH YES, ROY—IT'S SUPER. I'M HAVING A LOVELY TIME.

I couldn't believe it when she said she'd meet me again . . .

I was so amazed to be with her that I didn't even mind when other guys chatted her up . . .

YOU MUST GO OUT WITH LOTS OF GUYS, I MEAN, SOMEONE WELL—SO NICE . . .

THANKS—I DON'T DO BADLY, I SUPPOSE. BUT I'M PRETTY BUSY, TOO. I GO TO YOGA CLASSES AND I TAKE GERMAN AT NIGHT SCHOOL.

IT WON'T LAST, MATE. I MEAN, LOOK AT YOU—THERE ARE THOUSANDS OF BETTER-LOOKING GUYS AROUND, AND SHE COULD HAVE HER PICK.

BROUGHT YOU SOME PUNCH, ROSANNA . . .

HAVEN'T SEEN YOU FOR A WHILE. WHAT'VE YOU BEEN DOING?

FOLKS—I'D LIKE YOU TO MEET ROY.

. . . or when they danced with her . . .

Lucky? No guy could have been so lucky . . .

DANCE AS CLOSE AS YOU LIKE, PAL. I'M THE ONE WHO'S SEEING HER HOME . . .

NIGHT, FOLKS!

YOU LUCKY . . .

HEY—I'M THE LUCKY ONE!

THREE WEEKS—I CAN'T BELIEVE IT! SHE ACTUALLY LIKES GOING OUT WITH ME . . .

And after a few more weeks had passed . . .

To begin with it was great being envied by so many blokes . . .

But after a while I began to resent all the whistling and chatting up . . .

I GUESS YOU MUST KNOW MY FEELINGS, ROSANNA—I LOVE YOU, BUT—I MEAN, HOW DO YOU FEEL ABOUT ME?

OH, ROY—CAN'T YOU SEE? I'M WILD, MAD . . . NUTS ABOUT YOU!

WHISTLE ALL YOU LIKE, CHUMS. BUT SHE'S MINE! ISN'T THAT RIGHT, ROSANNA?

FOREVER, ROY!

SORRY, PAL—CONVERSATION OVER!

B-BUT, ROY . . .

Continued on page 62

HOW WOULD YOU LABEL YOURSELF?

*Everyone uses "labels" to describe people, but getting stuck with one is no fun. So take a look and see if **your** label is here, then find out how you can get rid of it!*

Flirting's an art, a teasing game. It's different from chatting up, because there's usually nothing at all serious about it, on either side. Flirting's as light as candy floss, and just as much fun — provided you know when to do it and where to stop.

There's nothing wrong in a little mutual admiration, fluttering your eyelashes at a boy, and letting him know you think he's pretty nice — provided you both know it's just a game and that the game has very strict rules!

Rules like not flirting with your boyfriend's mates to the extent that it makes him look a fool. Like not flirting at all if your boyfriend's the jealous, insecure type!

You have to be careful who you flirt with. Some boys take it all very seriously, and when they do eventually twig it's just a game,they're liable to feel cheated, angry and perhaps humiliated, too. They're the kind of boys who'll label you as a flirt — and sometimes even worse!

How important is your best friend? Is she high on your list of Very Important People?

Imagine yourself in this situation:

The boy you've drooled over for months has at last asked you out. You're all dressed up and halfway out the door to meet him when the phone rings. It's your best friend and she's in real trouble. She needs your help. Can you come round?

Agony!

If your answer's an emphatic "not-on-your-life" then you're only a fair-weather friend, and chances are none of your friendships are ever very deep or lasting because you tend to disappear when the going gets rough, or something better turns up.

We don't mean you should be a doormat! If you have a mate who expects you to drop everything every five minutes and switch plans because she wants attention, you'll have to be firm with her and not let her use you.

But if a friend really needs you, you ought to be able to make sacrifices, compromises and try your best to help — because that's what friends are for!

Like discos? Like eating out? Like boxes of chocolates in the cinema and nice pressies?

Well, there's nothing wrong with that, 'cos we all like having a good time, but you mustn't expect your guy to cough up *every* time, and you must *never* measure his love by how much he spends on you, because that would be putting a price tag on the relationship.

If you're going steady and are both on allowances, or both earning, it's only fair to share the cost of going out.

It's important to talk about money and work out how you're going to cope — there's nothing more embarrassing than standing behind two people in the cinema queue and listening to them squabble about whose turn it is!

A first date might seem a bit awkward. If he asks you out, he probably intends to pay for everything, so let him choose where you'll go. If he insists *you* choose, then get him to suggest a few things so that you've an idea of the kind of evening he has in mind.

It's nice to make a gesture towards paying your share, even on the first date, and the nicest way to do this is to buy the choc ices at the pictures, or the chips on the long walk home.

That way, no-one can ever accuse you of being a gold digger, or of being out for what you can get.

Moods can be an awful problem. Sometimes you know why you're miserable. Your boyfriend walked out on you, or you failed an important exam.

But sometimes, for no apparent reason, a black mood of depression can descend on you, and you feel like crying at the least little thing.

It's all part of growing up, but if you're having a hard time coping, it's easy to end up being picked on by brothers, sisters, or classmates, because people quickly realise that you always respond to teasing.

Things *will* improve, so remember that, and don't think you must be going mad.

See your doctor and make sure there's nothing wrong with your health.

This is important because no-one can cope with life's ups and downs when they're run down.

Make sure you get enough good food, fresh air, sleep and exercise.

If you're really miserable because you're being picked on, *tell someone*. Sharing your worry is half the battle, and knowing you're not alone will make you feel better right away.

Aim to keep busy, to occupy your mind so that you don't have time to brood. Gradually you'll start to feel less and less at the mercy of your moods and you'll begin to feel more able to cope with them. Learn to understand your moods, remember that everyone has them, especially whilst they're growing up, and try to control your temper — there's nothing worse than a *real* cry baby, who always uses tears to get her own way!   •

Your hair can be brown, black, red or even purple, but if you act thick, you'll quickly find yourself labelled a "dumb blonde."

Some girls act dumb, because they think it makes them seem frail, helpless and appealing. And maybe it does to King Kong types, or boys who like a "me-Tarzan-you-Jane" kind of relationship. But think about it — it's daft to get yourself into a situation where you're trapped into acting a part all the time.

No decent boy is going to be scared off because you're bright, interesting and have a mind of your own.

So read the papers, keep your eyes and ears open, and don't be afraid to ask lots of questions. That way you'll never be labelled a dummy!

A pushover isn't usually someone who's particularly easy-going. Often it's someone who's just a bit afraid to stick up for herself, in case she makes herself unpopular.

If you get the reputation of being a pushover, respect flies out of the window and friendships and romances become an uphill struggle.

So before you do what someone else wants you to do — think! Do you really want to do it? Or are you just afraid no-one will like you if you say no?

If it's the last, then take a deep breath and say no.

The world won't suddenly collapse around your ears. In fact, once you've learned to say no, you'll probably find the world's a much nicer place!

SCARY MONSTERS AND SUPER LEAPS!

Some of your favourite stars talk about the most dangerous thing they'd like to try . . .

LEWIS COLLINS would like to come down to earth in style!

"After trying parachuting, which was something I'd wanted to do ever since I can remember, the really frightening thing I'd like to try is a free fall," he said. "That's where you just let yourself fall through the air and don't open your parachute until the last minute. People who've done it say it's an incredible feeling!"

"The most terrible thing I can

think of," said **JOE JACKSON,** "is getting up before I have to!"

"I love racing cars," **NOEL EDMONDS** said, "and indulge myself whenever I get the chance. But the one thing I'd really like to do is race in the world famous Indianapolis 500 Race. It's one of the hairiest races there is!"

ZOOT ALORS of **THE PIRANHAS** seems to be a bit braver than most!

"I'd love to spend the night in a haunted building," he told us. "We actually used to rehearse in the basement of a church which was meant to be haunted, but I couldn't get up the nerve to win a bet and stay there all night by myself!"

"I'd put doing a loop the loop in an aeroplane at the top of my list,"

said **GARY NUMAN.** "I like flying, but to be able to do acrobatics, you would need nerves of steel!"

KATE BUSH would like to travel into the past.

"I'd like to try going to a hypnotist to see if I'd lived before," she confessed. "But there's a danger in it, because it's possible that the hypnotist might not be able to

bring you back to the present!"

"I wish I had the nerve to try hang-gliding," said **DAVID VAN DAY.** "I've been taking flying lessons and that doesn't scare me at all. But to jump off a hill with only a bit of material to hold me up, sends shivers up and down my spine!"

"The most dangerous and frightening thing I would like to try," said **THE ED.,** "is to face a crazed, hysterical mob all on my own and bring them under control. For example, I'd tell the Patches staff that they've all got to be in at nine or ELSE!"

Continued from page 59

THAT WAS RUDE!

AH, BUT YOU SHOULDN'T BE SO BEAUTIFUL—THEN I WOULDN'T HAVE THE SUDDEN URGE TO GET YOU ALONE.

LOVE ME?

MMM—OF COURSE I DO!

But each day made me more and more scared of losing her.

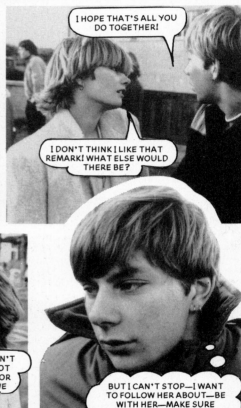

SOME GUYS ARE SO PERSISTENT—WHAT IF THERE'S SOMEBODY AT HER NIGHT CLASS, SOME GUY SHE MIGHT NOT BE ABLE TO RESIST?

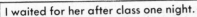

I waited for her after class one night.

SEE YOU, ROSANNA!

ROY, WHAT ARE YOU DOING HERE?

ER—HAD SOME SPARE TIME ON MY HANDS—THOUGHT I'D GET YOU HOME.

WHO'S THAT BLOKE? PRETTY FRIENDLY, ISN'T HE?

DAVE STEVENS—WE HELP EACH OTHER WITH GERMAN VERBS SOMETIMES.

I HOPE THAT'S ALL YOU DO TOGETHER!

I DON'T THINK I LIKE THAT REMARK! WHAT ELSE WOULD THERE BE?

I should have taken the warning but I just couldn't lay off—even when she was just going out with her friends . . .

I THOUGHT YOU'D PREFER MY COMPANY TO A LOT OF GABBLING GIRLS . . .

WHAT IF THEY GET IN TOW WITH SOME GUYS?

IT'S MY NIGHT OUT WITH MY FRIENDS, ROY, AND I'M NOT GOING TO CHANGE IT.

YOU'RE SPOILING THINGS. DON'T YOU KNOW THAT? YOU'VE GOT TO STOP BEING SO JEALOUS OR IT'LL BE ALL OVER BEFORE WE KNOW WHERE WE ARE.

Y-YEAH, YOU'RE RIGHT, ROSANNA. I'M SORRY!

BUT I CAN'T STOP—I WANT TO FOLLOW HER ABOUT—BE WITH HER—MAKE SURE NOBODY'S TRYING TO STEAL HER AWAY FROM ME . . .

There was just no way I could stop myself—and now, a few weeks later . . .

HI, DAVE! FANCY SEEING YOU HERE!

THAT'S THE GUY FROM HER GERMAN CLASS—I MUSTN'T SAY ANYTHING—I MUST KEEP MY COOL . . .

HI, ROSANNA. MAKES A CHANGE FROM GERMAN VERBS.

. . . BUT THE WAY THEY SMILED AT EACH OTHER. MAYBE THERE IS SOMETHING GOING ON BEHIND MY BACK . . ?

BIGGER-THAN-USUAL POP·WORD!

Everything's bigger in our first annual — and that includes the Pop-word! Just to help, we've filled in the centre line, so all you have to do is to find the answers to the clues. There're no prizes for this one, and you can find the answers on page 87. No peeking, though!

1	SNOW	P	LOUGHS
2	SNOWM	A	N
3	PAN	T	OMIMES
4	RONNIE	C	ORBETT
5	LARRY	H	AGMAN
6	ANNIE L	E	NNOX
7	JIMMY	S	AVILE
8	EDD	I	E KIDD
9	GLADY	S	KNIGHT
10	MISS PI	G	GY
11	ROCKFO	R	D FILES
12	KENNY	E	VERETT
13	GAMB	A	CCINI
14	CHRIS	T	MAS EVE
15	FUN	F	AIRS
16	ELVIS C	O	STELLO
17	CLIFF	R	ICHARD
18	PENELO	P	E KEITH
19	RUDOLP	H	
20	TERRY W	O	GAN
21	PRESEN	T	S
22	ROBIN C	O	USINS
23	THE	S	HADOWS
24	FAWLTY	T	OWERS
25	SN	O	WBALLS
26	ANGELA	R	IPPON
27	DEBB	I	E HARRY
28	HAPPY N	E	W YEAR
29	ISLA	S	T. CLARE

1. These vehicles clear the snow from roads (11).
2. You can only build this guy in winter (7).
3. Traditional shows at Christmas-time (10).
4. The smaller of the Two Ronnies (6, 7).
5. JR! (5, 6).
6. She sang with The Tourists (5, 6).

7. Jim'll Fix It! (5, 6).
8. Britain's answer to Evel Knievel (5, 4).
9. This American singer is backed by The Pips (6, 6).
10. This Muppet has a green boyfriend! (4, 5).
11. This American TV detective series starred James Garner (8, 5).
12. The guy with the crazy Video Show (5, 7).
13. Radio 1's American DJ, Paul (10).
14. The night Santa comes to visit! (9, 3).
15. They've got roundabouts, shooting galleries and coconut shies (8).
16. No, not Presley. This one's English and he's got Attractions! (5, 8).
17. Harry Webb has been in pop for over 20 years (5, 7).
18. She was Margo in "The Good Life" (8, 5).
19. The reindeer with the colourful hooter! (7).
20. The Radio 2 DJ who hosts "Blankety Blank" (5, 5).
21. What you give and receive on Christmas Day (8).
22. British World Champion ice-skater (5, 7).
23. Hank Marvin's in this group which used to back No. 17 (3, 7).
24. John Cleese owns this hotel on TV (6, 6).
25. These get thrown around when it snows! (9).
26. BBC's first female newsreader (6, 6).
27. Blondie's blonde (6, 5).
28. What you say to everyone on January 1 (5, 3, 4).
29. Larry Grayson's Saturday girl (4, 2, 5).

A week in the life of...
DEBBIE HARRY

Debbie Harry's diary is a busy one, and here's just one week from it!

SATURDAY

Chris and I are at home in Manhattan and the weather's cold and icy. We put the central heating on even though it's making a heck of a noise. Been playing some records real low because I've got a pile of film scripts that I'm trying to wade through to see if there's anything suitable for me.

It can be interesting and exciting if the script is good, even if it is unsuitable, and terribly boring if it isn't.

We're eating at home today.

Debbie in concert.

SUNDAY

Clem is in the middle of sketching out ideas for his new book on drumming. He told me he'd been ringing around to ask a few people their opinions, and talking to other drummers about ideas. He thinks it'd be good for aspiring musicians and he's having a lot of fun writing it.

Me and Chris are planning to take a break and fly to Los Angeles.

MONDAY

Chris and I make definite arrangements for the flight to the West Coast. Let's hope that things are a lot warmer there than they are in New York. Went for a meal in Greenwich Village, took a cab there. Sure wish someone would fix those giant potholes in the road, they certainly shake you about a lot. It's freezing so we don't spend too much time wandering around.

TUESDAY

Jimmy is here in New York and spending a lot of time helping new bands by giving them advice and producing records for them. Chris is doing the same thing and has been down to the studio putting the finishing touches to a group's single. Chris says that he finds it rewarding helping new bands get a foot on the ladder to the charts.

I went out to have a look round some of the stores. Haven't been able to do that for a long time and it was a bit of a luxury.

WEDNESDAY

People say that Chris and I don't go out to small clubs much, but that's not really true. In fact, tonight we're off to a club to listen to some unknown bands. If they're any good, Chris might be able to offer them some help.

Meanwhile I went to see the girl who designs most of my clothes for me. I wanted to discuss some new ideas with her and that's always exciting.

THURSDAY

Spent most of the morning packing our gear for the flight to Los Angeles. It'll be a nice break. Took a cab to the airport and bought an armload of magazines to read during the flight. After all the film scripts, it should be nice and relaxing.

Debbie and Chris at home.

Chris.

FRIDAY

In Los Angeles at last! We were met by friends at the airport. It seems such a total change from New York. Although we're officially on holiday, I intend having some discussions with film producers about the scripts I've been reading. Hope to listen to some of the West Coast sounds in the clubs, too!

LOS ANGELES HOLLYWOOD

Frank Infanti, Nigel Harrison, Debbie, Jimmy Destri, Chris Stein and Clem Burke.

SHOWSTOPPERS!

GOLDEN GIRL: Keep it casual, fun and easy. Simple gold accessories with a plain khaki outfit make it easier on your pocket, too. Not too fussy, but suitable for lots of different occasions. You're a cheerful, friendly girl — always up to something. You don't like to spend too much time on dressing up, but you like to look good.

NEW ROMANTIC: Make it sweet, but add a touch of mystery. Lace and ruffles, soft fabrics and colours, too. Just think romance! You're an imaginative, fantasy-loving girl and you like to stand out in a crowd. You set the styles which create the most impact!

We thought we'd stage our very own fashion show, featuring the most popular looks from 1981, and then let the guys tell us what they really thought! Find out a little about yourself, too, by choosing your favourite outfit and then comparing notes with our "judges!"

SIXTIES MISS: Really groovy! Minis, cardis and bright bold jewellery put this look together. A simple hairband keeps your hairstyle in check while you get into the groove. What a swingin' chick! You're probably slightly off-beat and love to wear clothes which others will instantly recognise as being from a specific era. Basically, you love all clothes, but especially things which reflect your carefree attitude.

DISCO-DANCER: Looking like a million dollars. Very cool, and oh, so sophisticated! In gear like this, you'll dance the rest of the disco off their feet. You're definitely a sophisticated type — you go for luxury and style in your life — when you can get 'em! You probably project a cool, distant image, though underneath you're a fairly level-headed sort of girl, who's got everything worked out!

Continued overleaf

Continued from previous page

COWGIRL: Lots of denim, checks, studded belts, cowboy boots and huge Stetsons — and you're home on the range. Even J.R.'d be impressed! You like to turn heads — not because you want to shock, but because you're slightly mad! You like to dress up for a giggle — any style taken to extremes suits you — and there's no harm in that!

RED INDIAN: HOW!? It's easy . . . feathers and fringes with everything. On the dress, the bag and the shoes. Pocahontas had nothing on this! You're quite a romantic at heart and would love to have been a wild Red Indian, roaming on the plains. You like the softness of this kind of outfit, too, which reflects your gentle personality.

1. Khaki boiler suit from Freemans Catalogue. Gold bag from Way In at Harrods. Gold belt, bangles, earrings, and hair clasp by Beau Jangles. Gold pumps from Dolcis.

2. White blouse by Jeffrey Rogers. Black lacy skirt worn as shawl, by Johnsons. Pink mini kilt by Brand X. Black stirrup tights from the Dance Centre. White boots, from Saxone. Pink feather brooch from Way In at Harrods.

3. Beige cardigan and red skirt from Top Shop. Red hair-band and red brooch by Beau Jangles. Black shoes from Curtess. Tights and beads, model's own.

4. Silk print trousers and jacket by Jeff Banks. Boob tube from Chelsea Girl. Gold belt from Way In at Harrods. Mules by Terry de Havilland. Blue necklace from Way In at Harrods. Half-moon earrings by Beau Jangles.

5. Checked shirt by Gloria Vanderbilt. Hat from Take Six. Brooch by Beau Jangles. Belt by Trimfit. Skirt by Paul Howie. Boots from Sacha.

6. Lilac dress from Top Shop. Grey belt from Way In at Harrods. Feather comb from Way In at Harrods. Grey feather hairslide by Beau Jangles. Pink fringed bag from Top Shop. Wooden beads by Beau Jangles. Moccasins from Freeman Hardy Willis.

Now that you've seen the show, let's go over to our judges, to find out what they had to say about the six outfits . . .

PETER-PAUL

(Model)

1. Golden Girl — One word springs to mind — starts with an S and ends with a Y . . . SLOPPY! I've seen better things crawling out of . . . (unrepeatable, Ed.) Only fit for tearing up and cleaning the windows with! (Who'd ever guess that Peter-Paul didn't like this? Ed.)

2. New Romantic — This lacks the individuality New Romantics supposedly strive for. Probably a Visage or Spandau Ballet fan. Back to the drawin' board, darlin'!

3. Sixties Miss — Aaaaagh! Big yawn. Wheel the next one in . . .!

4. Disco Dancer — The best of the six outfits. I like the large shoulders and the striking paintbox pattern. The white would show up wonderfully under ultra-violet lighting. Fun to wear yet slightly sophisticated . . . definitely for the girl who wants to get noticed. I bet those high heels are killing her, though!

5. Cowgirl — She looks as if she's been shot at and hit!

6. Red Indian — Dressed like that, I'd suggest she stays in her wigwam. Such a pity . . . seems like a nice girl!

GARY

(Model)

1. Golden Girl — I've always found khaki drab and uninteresting. It has little character. This outfit is my runner-up for the worst look.

2. New Romantic — This looks rather like a hotchpotch of what was left over from the jumble sale, and the boots from the Sixties girl. Never mind, love!

3. Sixties Miss — What has the cat dragged in! This is such old hat, the second time round. I don't know why her mother doesn't ask for her clothes back!

4. Disco Dancer — This is very pleasant and I'd find it a treat to walk down the street with my girl wearing this colourful outfit.

5. Cowgirl — Oh, the farmer and the cowgirl should be friends . . . (y'what? Ed.) I could appreciate

someone wearing this on 31st December at 12 o'clock, otherwise, ''Bang, you're dead!''

6. Red Indian — This is a pretty little dress from the opposite camp to No. 5. Suitable for various occasions and probably the most conventional.

Unfortunately this is all we could get out of Suggs and Bedders, from Madness. The cowgirl seemed to be their favourite, but we reckon they were too overcome by the other stunning outfits to say much more . . . speechless, perhaps?!

SUGGS

I like the backdrop! Those long boots could catch on.

BEDDERS

I like the skirt. She's got a great pair of legs — I don't like the rest!

So now you know . . .

ARE YOU INTRO, EXTRO OR

How's your mind today? Are you feeling outrageous,
kind of person you are, try our soulful quiz, and

1. In which of these houses do you think you'd find perfect peace and happiness?

a

b

c

d

2. Someone — or something — is leaning on the window-sill, staring out. The world's out there — freedom — all you've got to do is leap softly to the grass and walk to the river. There're wild horses there, galloping with the wind in their manes. Beyond that, gleaming white mountain peaks pierce the sky . . .
Who's this story about? Who is dreaming of freedom?

a   b   c   d

3. It's a summer afternoon. You're lying on the grass, the air's soft on your face, birds are singing, and the warm sun lulls you to drowsiness. These clouds drift by. What pictures do you see in them?

a. *An ornate boat ready to set sail for a voyage of discovery.*
b. *Somebody galloping along on a horse – a long cloak flowing behind them.*
c. *Scarey monsters.*
d. *A giant jar filled with jube-jubes, dolly mixtures and other goodies.*

JUST INBETWEENO?

PATCHES QUIZ

daring or just plain dozy? If you'd like to find out what

discover what makes you tick!

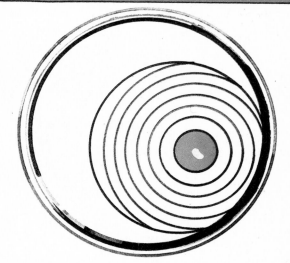

6. You are alone, walking along a tunnel. It's dark, the sound of your frightened breathing and your quickening footsteps echo round you. Suddenly, in front of you — there's an orange glow. What is it?
a. Sunshine, fresh air and freedom.
b. Another tunnel, only orange.
c. A light orange room filled with your enemies.
d. A giant fried egg.

4. Fill in the balloon. What's she saying to him?
a. Gosh, you're attractive. What's your name?
b. You're standing on my toe.
c. It's over! I'm leaving you.
d. I'm the Daily Bugle's sunshine supergirl. And you've just won £5.

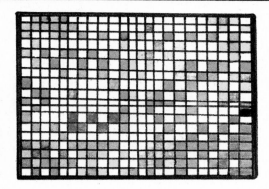

5. What do these squares suggest to you?
a. Adam making Antmusic.
b. A lot of little squares.
c. A number 57.
d. The telly's on the blink.

7. What is this girl doing?
a. She's got an ice cube up her sleeve and is trying to catch it.
b. Putting something high on a shelf.
c. Fending off an attacker.
d. The hokey-cokey.

8. What's this?
a. A doughnut.
b. A wedding ring.
c. A lifebelt.
d. A hoop to train goldfish to jump through.

You've delved into the darkest recesses of your mind, swept the cobwebs to the wind, bared your soul. It's the big moment now!
To find out how you've done, turn to page 73, if you dare!

Continued from previous page

CONCLUSIONS:

If you scored mostly a's: You are basically extrovert. You like folk, and, generally speaking, folk like you back again. It's really a very healthy attitude. The only thing that might be wrong is that you have to keep a constant chatter going, because you don't like being alone with yourself.

You don't like to examine the secret you, you don't like to come too close to your private hopes and dreams and fears. You're scared to hope and dream in case you get disappointed, and thinking about your deep fears terrifies you! If you confess a few of these things you'll find that everybody feels the same at times and talking things over will help you all!

Mostly b's: You're a practical soul. You like everything in its place and hate too many frills and fancies. It's annoying being practical, isn't it? You'd rather read that you were a wistful romantic. You wish when someone suggests a picnic in the rain you didn't immediately think it would just mean you ending up with the flu. You wish you didn't have that small, extremely sane voice in the back of your head.

But being practical needn't be rotten, and being sensible doesn't make you automatically stodgy and boring. You can have the best of both worlds if you try. You can be funny, wear outrageous clothes and dance all night — and still have that strong streak of commonsense that makes you a well-balanced person.

Mostly c's: Ah-ha, an introvert. Well, that's the swift way of putting it. You enjoy being an introvert, don't you? Prone to moods and black depressions one moment, extreme highs the next. You've got yourself a reputation for being a bit strange. Not exactly a weirdo, but people think you're a bit mysterious. Also they imagine you have great depths. Well, who'd do anything to discourage people from thinking that!

Only don't overdo it. Try not to indulge in your mysteriousness too much or you'll baffle your pals, and they'll eventually leave you to your own devices. Then you really *will* be alone.

Mostly d's: Well now! Obviously we had to consult many, many books for this quiz — "The Origin Of Species," "The Psychology Of Modern Youth," "Teenagers — Why Do They Wear Striped Socks?", "People Under Twenty And Their Relationships With Digestive Biscuits" and so on. All vital and important books.

It was put together by a team of psychologists, doctors, social workers, sociologists, banana importers and school dinner ladies. We made an intensive study of hundreds of different tribes and races and can come to only one conclusion. You're extremely silly — like us!

DETECT A FELLA!

Winter's a time for disappearing. The sun disappears, the leaves disappear, the insects disappear—and so do boys! So warm up your woollies, button up your balaclava—and start hunting!

A LOT of girls seem to get the idea that boys hibernate like hedgehogs during the winter months. Some girls even go out into the country to look under bushes and turn over stones in the hope of finding a sleeping boy. But all they find are last year's discarded Coke cans and the occasional frog. Sad, isn't it?

The truth is that boys *don't* hibernate in the winter months. They only appear to. The cold weather tends to make them sluggish, and they have a habit of huddling together in warm places.

The dedicated Winter Boy Hunter must first find out where these places are. Cynthia Prune, a part-time boiled egg tapper, from Wigan, trained a pack of dogs to seek out hidden boys.

Now boys generally do their winter huddling in the warmest caffs, coffee bars and youth club table tennis and snooker rooms. In Wigan, it didn't matter where they were, Cynthia's dogs would find them.

Unfortunately, although she found dozens of huddled boys, she didn't actually get a chance to get to know any of them. This was because her dogs

were very fierce.

The arrival of Cynthia and her pack of snarling, barking dogs at any caff/coffee bar/ youth club, would cause instant panic among the huddled boys, and they would leap out of windows and even climb up chimneys in their hurry to escape.

So don't try Cynthia's system. Be more subtle. Get together with some other dedicated Winter Boy Hunters and send out search parties until you've pinpointed the huddled boys' hideouts.

Then all you have to do is go round to all the places with pins stuck in them until you've found the right boy for you.

BUT, as he'll be busy huddling and shivering and talking to his mates about motor-bikes, football and electric blankets, how are you going to get him to notice you? Boys don't take half as much notice of girls in winter as they do in summer.

Maybe it's because, with your thick winter woollies on, the guys aren't sure you *are* a girl. Boys are a bit simple sometimes.

The secret is to get yourself noticed. In a caff or coffee bar order a hot Coke with tomato

for rescuing him. If you aren't lucky — you won't.

Try the sledge assault system instead. This is quite simple. All you need is a sledge. If you haven't got one, swipe your kid brother's or bribe someone to lend you theirs.

Then find a hill which has a number of boys fooling around on it. Climb to the top of the hill, select the guy you fancy most and swoop down the hill on him on your sledge at ninety miles an hour.

All you have to do then, after the impact, is help him to his feet, apologising breathlessly and explaining that you're really not very good at sledging. Unless he's badly injured or in shock, he'll jump at the opportunity of teaching a helpless girl the finer arts of sledging and you'll have him hooked.

OR borrow a small child and encourage him or her to cry loudly while you awkwardly pile up a mound of snow. "He won't stop crying until I've built him a snowman," you explain to the nearest gorgeous guy, "and I'm hopeless."

Gorgeous guy will start showing off his snowman-building skills, and by the time he's finished, you should be good for a date or two. Or even a currant.

Or arrive at the local pond with a pair of ice skates and a sign that reads "Danger. Thin Ice!" Stick the sign in the pond when nobody is looking and then start strapping on your skates. If the scheme works, some nice guy will come over and point out the notice. You can thank him warmly for saving your life and, again, you should have him hooked.

So don't sit indoors all winter, wishing it was spring. Get out there and join the Great Patches Winter Boy Hunt!

The guys are out there somewhere — all you've got to do is find them. And the rest is up to you!

sauce in a loud voice. This should attract attention and might make the boy you're after curious enough to ask you why you're drinking a mixture like that.

"It's all the rage in Ashby-de-la-Zouch," you can explain casually, or, "I don't like tomato sauce, so I have it mixed with Coke to hide the taste."

Of course, this scheme won't work too well if everybody in the place is drinking hot Coke with tomato sauce. If they are, get out quick — they're a load of loonies!

Another way to attract the attention of the boy you're keen on, is to turn up with your leg in plaster. Not many boys can resist writing their names on plaster casts. And the sight of you hobbling about might also wake him up enough for him to help you to your chair. If you've really roused his gentlemanly instincts, he might even carry you home.

Or turn up with an unusual pet on a lead. A penguin, maybe, or a vulture, or an ant.

Or arrive wearing a sweater embroidered with the words; "I'm not doing anything special tonight. Any offers?"

THE only times boys *do* wake up and actually get out and about, are when it's snowing and when there's a football match on.

Boys tend to enjoy playing football, whatever the weather. It's difficult to see why. They end up bruised and covered with mud, but if that's their idea of fun . . .

You can make yourself popular by turning up at a match wearing the local team colours and cheering madly. Some guy or other is sure to spot you, especially as, at this time of year, you're likely to be the only spectator there. You might even make all your friends jealous by being the only girl around with eleven boyfriends and two reserves.

But the best time for the dedicated Winter Boy Hunter is when the snow is on the ground. Boys are just big kids at heart, and you'll find them everywhere — throwing snowballs, zooming down hills on sledges and generally making fools of themselves.

You can make a start by searching snowdrifts. If you're lucky you might find some delectable guy who's been trapped in one for days, and he'll be terribly grateful to you

73

I WISH I'D SAID THAT!

WHEN your boyfriend comes out with a really cutting comment, are you ready right away with a cool, snappy reply — or do you just start throwing things? We've come up with a few tips on how to come out on top every time simply by knowing what to say — and when!

Y'know the situation. You and he are in the middle of a row that blew up over nothing at all. Suddenly, he turns round and yells, "I'm sick of the way you go on nagging! None of my mates have this problem!"

Instead of coming out with a snappy, put-down remark that'll bring him back to his normal, nice senses, you promptly burst into tears and rush out of the room saying you never want to see him again!

Familiar picture? We've all gone through it. It's only afterwards, when you're fuming into your box of tissues upstairs, that you think of cutting little come-backs like, "Well, none of your mates are going out with *you,* are they?" Or, "There isn't a problem! Just leave!" Or, "I know you're sick! Maybe you should see a doctor!"

If he's really being rotten, then that kind of backchat can take the wind out of his sails and shut him up for long enough to get the situation back in perspective and avoid a senseless row.

But what about the sort of situation where *you* know perfectly well he *has* seen you holding hands with Jimmy Thomson at the back of the disco? If you want to get rid of him, just admit it and walk back to Jimmy. But if you want to keep him, you'll have to bluff your way out of it!

"I know, isn't it sad?" you can begin to murmur, eyes shining with tears. "Poor Jimmy. It's such a shame. He needed someone to talk to. I'd love to tell you everything, but you know me — I always

keep secrets. Even from the guy I love!" Then you throw your arms round his neck and give him a big kiss! This should all confuse him so much he'll drop the subject of you and Jimmy — which'll let you breathe again!

Trouble comes, of course, all the time — like when you've just bought what you consider to be *the* most amazing bright orange, towelling track-suit covered in

black zips!

He takes one look at it and thoughtfully tells you that you look exactly like a carrot with black-fly!

Now, if you've just spent a fortune on this outfit, and he's started being sarcastic about it, you need to counter-attack!

"I didn't know carrots got black-fly. I thought they got root-fly which can only be cured by a spring dusting of Aldrin round the young plants," you can murmur casually, whilst adjusting your zips. (This nifty piece of information is something to file at the back of your mind, just in case somebody *does* say you look like a carrot with black-fly!)

He is likely to stare at you in open-mouthed astonishment — simply because you've very calmly and quietly given him a piece of totally irrelevant information without losing your temper!

Once he's had time to think, he'll probably start off on another tack.

"You're not actually going to go out in that, are you?" he'll laugh sarcastically.

"No," you can smile sweetly. "I'm wearing it to sleep in. Goodnight!" At which point you leave the room *without* slamming the door!

If all he's objecting to is your new outfit, he'll follow you inside five minutes and start apologising.

So, in a situation like that, never, ever lose your temper (however much you feel like hitting him over the head with a flower vase!) — and don't resort to criticising *his* appearance, either. Comments on his taste in sweat-shirts or socks are only going to blow the whole thing up into a slanging match between you!

Then there's the time when he appears forty minutes late for a date, looking sheepish and asking if you've been waiting long!

Pushing him under a passing bus isn't the answer here! Saying no, you've only just arrived yourself could lead to an argument as to why *you* were forty minutes late, and starting a whole long questionnaire on where he's been and with whom will only ruin the evening completely.

Try being sarcastic instead.

Tell him you actually *like* watching traffic and you're thinking of taking up collecting car numbers.

Inform him you've only been waiting long enough for several passers-by to mistake your handbag for a litter-bin and dump their toffee wrappers in it.

Smile sweetly, take his arm and murmur that *of course* forty minutes isn't long — it's only 2 point 7777777 per cent. of a day, and that isn't much between friends, is it? (You can always go on, thoughtfully, to add that that is only point 739726 per cent. of a year, which is hardly any time at all!) If he gives you a fairly dumb look — which he's quite likely to do — you can squeeze his arm playfully and tell him that working all that out made the minutes until he turned up slip past quite quickly, everything considered!

But there is one set of circumstances where saying the best thing and behaving in the right way is *always* difficult — and that's when he's handing you the old, "goodbye, it was fun" line.

If you haven't been expecting it, it's going to come as an awful shock, and on the spur of the moment, there's likely to be very little you can do about it except sit there and say, "Why?" in a plaintive voice.

He will then waffle on with all sorts of weird and wonderful explanations from how he's got to start spending more time with his piranha fish to the fact that his mother wants him in every night at eight o'clock! One guy out of ten will give the *real* reason — that he's bored, found somebody else, or just wants to flirt around a bit.

So if he starts on about how he's got to brush up his Swahili before he takes his "O"-levels, fix him with a sweet smile and say, "I understand. Kwaheri." Then leave, before you burst into tears! (Kwaheri actually *means* "Goodbye" in Swahili!) He might be so intrigued by this that he'll come after you to find out what you meant! If he doesn't, resign yourself to the fact that it *is* over — and go home and have a good cry!

If you don't know any Swahili, or he's come up with another equally feeble excuse for ending it all — don't start to argue with him. Thank him for all the good times. Tell him you'll miss him. Ask him

if he wants the Police albums he gave you for your birthday back. Say you suppose you'll have to throw away that lock of his hair you've been keeping in your locket and kissing every night. Wish him every success and happiness, very formally, by shaking his hand. In other words, leave him feeling an utter, low-down, unlikeable *heel,* without actually calling him that!

But if you *have* suspected for a while that perhaps he was teetering on the edge of a farewell scene, at least you've had time to think how you'll behave, and plan things out.

As he starts to mutter and mumble and scrape his feet along the floor, pat him on the arm and ask him sympathetically if his ingrowing toe-nail (or whatever!) is playing him up again.

"Not exactly," he'll probably mutter.

"You really *should* have that seen to, you know," you can chirp on cheerfully. "I once heard of somebody who lost their whole *leg* because of an ingrown toe-nail." (Or their whole head, or arm, or whichever other part of his anatomy's been worrying him!)

Now, it's a sad, but true fact of life that nearly *all* guys are hypochondriacs — they sneeze because they've got dust up their noses and immediately decide they're dying of pneumonia!

Yours is unlikely to be an exception — and if you sympathetically (and wickedly, because *you* know what you're doing. *He* doesn't!) steer him on to the subject of his health, he'll get so worried about himself, and be so grateful to you for being so kind — he'll forget all *about* what he's originally started out to say!

Getting the last word *always* makes you feel better. But finding the last word at the precise moment you *need* it isn't easy.

There's the sort of situation where he's with a crowd of his mates and is busily going on about how you can never make up your mind about anything.

"On yes, I can," you smile. "It's just that *my* mind isn't the same as your mind — it's better!"

Or, if he's being really rude and rotten and tells you to drop dead, you can counter-attack with, "Don't be silly! Women live longer than men! *Everybody* knows that!"

Or if he suddenly wrinkles his nose and demands, "What's that nasty smell?" (when he knows perfectly well it's your new perfume because you've been telling him about it for twenty minutes!) — pause, sniff the air seriously, then murmur, "Your after-shave, I think!"

And one of the most beautiful put-downs of all, particularly at the end of an argument or when you *never* want to see him again — if he says something along the lines of, "Now tell me I'm right!", look him straight in the eye and, without smiling say, "Why should I bother? You're obviously convinced you are!"

Other good interchanges include:

HIM: Now I feel a fool! (After he's been proved wrong about something.)

YOU: Yes, you look a fool.

HIM: Why can't you ever be on time?

YOU: Why don't you buy me that watch I want?

HIM: Why d'you have to wash your hair *every* Wednesday?

YOU: Why not?

HIM: You think more of your cat/dog/budgie/stereo than you do of me.

YOU: *It* thinks more than you do!

HIM: I don't even *like* Dawn Williams! (When you know he fancies her like mad!)

YOU: Mmm. Funny! She said the same about you!

Y'see, it's all a matter of quick thinking! And there is one *other* situation where a handy quip at the right time can shut a whole *bunch* of fellas up!

That's when you suddenly discover you have to walk past about six of them, who all start shouting and whistling at you.

Muttering, "Drop dead!" under your

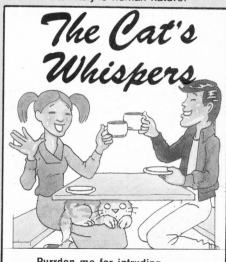

breath will just make matters worse, because that's what they're *expecting* you to say. They're also expecting you to rush on blindly, blushing like mad, and with any luck (from their point of view!) tripping over your feet!

Instead, slow down. Walk calmly. Don't look at them. Once they're within earshot, fix the whistling ones with a pleasantly sarcastic smile and murmur, "How nice! Joining a choir?" — then walk on.

At least they'll go quiet for thirty seconds!

And that's the main secret of finding the words to suit the occasions.

You don't *really* want to be nasty, or cruel, or arrogant. You just want to shut whoever's having a go at you up — for long enough to let *them* think what they've said and done!

Sometimes it works — and the person apologises.

Sometimes it doesn't — and the row or argument gets even worse.

But whatever happens, at least you've got the satisfaction of knowing that, for once, you *did* give as good as you got! Which isn't a particularly *nice* way of looking at life.

But it definitely *is* human nature!

The Cat's Whispers

Purrdon me for intruding . . .

SAVE ENERGY—

*We'd all like to look slim and be fit — it's getting that way that's the problem!
So we've worked out these fun exercises for you to do with your guy — or your
best friend! Who said exercising was a bore?!*

KNEEL AND ROCK

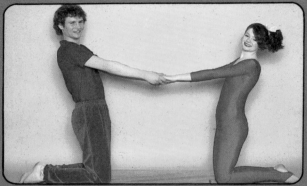

A. Kneel down facing each other. Hold hands straight out in front at waist level.

B. Move your body to one side until your bottom touches the floor, still holding your partner's hands (he remains still). Pull yourself up to the starting position again.

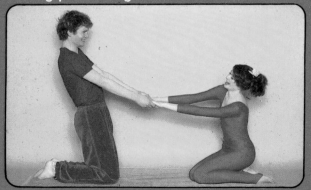

C. Now you sit in the starting position while he moves to one side.
Repeat the exerr 'se 5 times to each side. This is good for your stomach, legs and hips.

BACK TO BACK

A. Sit on the floor, backs together, legs in front and arms linked round your guy's at the elbows. Now bend your knees and start pressing against his back.

B. Slowly stand up together, still pressing against each other's back for support and slowly bringing your feet in towards your partner's.

C. Once you've reached the standing position, do the exercise again in reverse, ending up sitting on the ground again. Repeat 5 times. This is good for your tummy and your thighs.

EXERCISE WITH A FRIEND!

KNEE BENDS

A. Stand together, back to back, arms by sides.

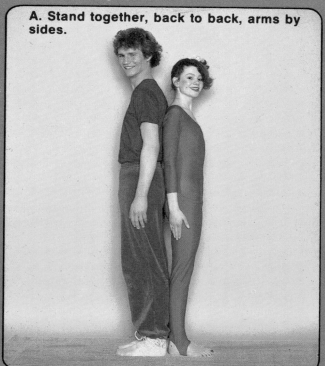

B. Slowly lower yourself to the ground, keeping your heels on the floor for as long as possible until you reach a squatting position.

C. Once squatting, bounce up and down together a few times, staying on your toes. Slowly rise to standing position again and repeat 5 times. This is good for back, thigh and calf muscles.

Continued on page 80

BE DEMURE IN THE DAYTIME...

Take one girl, add some basic make-up and get two different looks!

Lindsey's make-up begins with the foundation — Boots 17's Deluxe Moisture Rich Make-Up in Silky Ivory gives the right base. This is followed by Pressed Powder in Translucent. Finally, Deluxe Shimmering Blush Compact in Bramble Frost gives her face that lovely shape.

On to the eyes next! The Singles range is used — Lilac Wine on the lid, Purple Haze as the contour, and In The Pink for the highlighter. The eyes are completed with Thicklash mascara in Very Brown.

To finish the look off — Gleamer Lipstick in Fuchsia Flame and she's ready to face anything.

AND DAZZLE AT NIGHT

To make sure your purse isn't stretched too far, the same make-up is used for this basis. Silky Ivory foundation, Translucent powder and Bramble Frost blusher.

It's a special night out so the eyes are given some extra sparkle. Using Deluxe Silky Shadow, Turtle Dove goes on the inner eye and Chinchilla on the outer eye. Glitterbugs in Silver goes over the Chinchilla. To accentuate the eye, Kohl Brow and Lid Liner in Soft Black is used, finishing off with Thicklash Mascara in Very Brown.

Almost ready — Gleamer Lipstick in Cherry Brandy completes the picture and Lindsey's ready for the disco!

Make-up by Jo for Boots 17.

Continued from page 77

SIT-UPS
A. Lie on the floor, legs straight out in front of you, hands clasped behind your head.

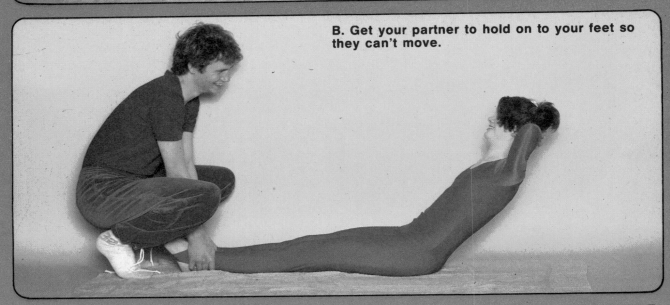

B. Get your partner to hold on to your feet so they can't move.

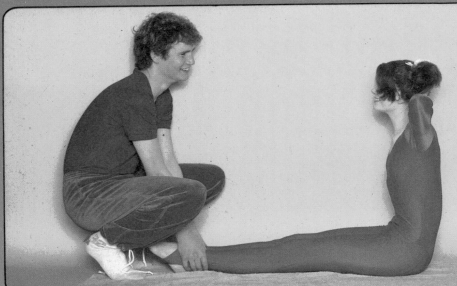

C. Slowly sit up, raising head and shoulders, as far as you can without raising your legs. Lie back down again slowly. Swap positions with your partner, and this time you act as the anchor. This is great for firming tummy and thigh muscles.

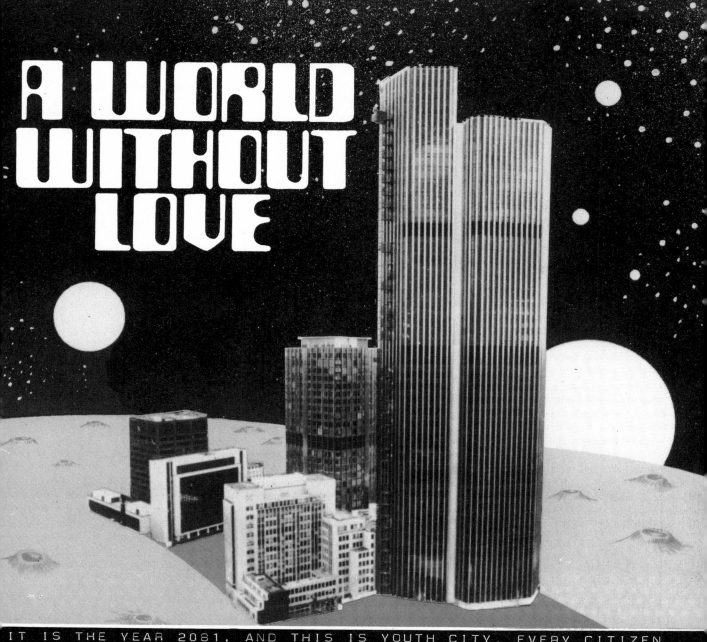

A WORLD WITHOUT LOVE

IT IS THE YEAR 2081, AND THIS IS YOUTH CITY. EVERY CITIZEN HERE IS UNDER TWENTY YEARS OF AGE, AND THERE ARE OLDER GOVERNMENT OFFICIALS TO SUPERVISE AND POLICE THEM...

...And generally tell them what to do.

IT'S A SHAME THE OLD VIDEO LIBRARY IS BEING DEMOLISHED—TRUST ME TO GET THE JOB OF CLEARING IT OUT. IT'LL BE A REAL BORE.

I'VE GOT TO CLEAR UP AND RE-FILE THIS ENTIRE FLOOR, BUT WHERE'S THE PERSON WHO'S SUPPOSED TO BE HELPING ME?

—EXCUSE ME...

Continued on page 84

Playing Cupid

Cast *in order of appearance:* **Fiona, Diane, Adam, Chris**

ACT ONE,

SCENE ONE:

A crowded, smoky disco. Near the juke box.

"Don't look now, but he's just come in and sat down!" Fiona says.

"*Who's* just sat down?" Diane says.

"Don't give me that — you know who I mean! *Him* — Chris Gates!"

"So?"

"So I saw you looking at him the other night, staring him out. I know you fancy him!"

"I do not!" Diane says heatedly. (*Too* heatedly, perhaps?) "I've never seen him before in my life. I haven't been staring at him at all!"

"All right, all right," Fiona says, with a maddening, knowing grin. "Have it your own way. Honestly, I don't know why you're so funny about me knowing that you fancy him. Anyone would think that . . ."

"I do *not* fancy him!"

"Sorry — I forgot. We'd better talk about something else before we come to blows. Did you see that red dress in Neon's window . . .?"

SCENE 2

— Other side of same disco.

"I see she's here tonight again, then," Adam says.

"Who?" Chris says.

"That girl who keeps staring at you — Diane something or other."

Chris shrugs. "Never heard of her."

Adam gives a roar of laughter. "Oh yeah? Couldn't figure out why you were so keen to miss football practice tonight — now I know!"

"Oh, go and take a jump!" Chris says rudely. "I don't know what you're talking about."

"I suppose you guessed that she'd be here again."

"I've never even *seen* her before!"

"Well, take a look now, then — she's over there by the juke box. Diane and her mate Fiona, giggling away like mad, probably planning to get hold of you later."

Chris peers through the smoke. "Never set eyes on her before in my life. Anyway, she's not my type."

SCENE 3

— The girls' side.

"He just looked over here — he did!" Fiona squeaks.

"So?"

"He craned his neck right round and *stared* at you. He obviously knows that you fancy him like mad!"

"I do *not*! I've only seen him a couple of times and what I've seen I don't fancy at all. In fact, I'm beginning to take a positive dislike to him. He's just not my type."

"You're just saying that . . ."

"And if you keep on about him I'm going home. *I don't like him!*"

"OK, OK, keep your hair on!"

SCENE 4

— The boys' side.

"Oh, they've really got you taped. You ought to see them sitting there, plotting away!"

"Leave off!"

"Shouldn't be surprised if she comes over in a minute and pretends to fall over in front of us or something. They always pull that sort of trick."

"I'll look the other way," Chris says moodily. "I told you, I don't like the look of her. Those girls are all the same, the way they run after anything in trousers. A fella's life isn't his own any more."

"You're telling me . . . Wait! They're looking in their purses. *Bet* they come over wanting change or something. Yeah! Diane's getting up!"

"I'm off!" Chris says. "They're not making a fool out of me. I'll come back when the coast's clear."

And at a gallop he sets off through the crowd in the direction of the bar at the back of the disco.

SCENE 5

— The girls' side.

"You go and phone for a taxi, then, and I'll keep this table," Fiona says.

"What time shall I say?"

"Ten thirty. Go round to the phone booth at the side where Chris is sitting."

"No, I won't! If that's the only one in here then I'm not going to phone at all!" Diane says, sitting down again.

"All right, touchy! Go to the one at the back, then — in the bar. Hurry up!"

SCENE 6

— At the bar.

"Ouch!"

"Why don't you look where you're going!"

"Oh, it's you!" Diane says, blinking up at Chris.

He puts out a hand to steady her and they stare at each other. As they do so, Something Happens, though right then they don't know what.

"I — I saw you the other night," Chris says.

"I saw you, too."

"Your name's Diane, isn't it?"

"And yours is Chris. My — my friend told me," Diane says, going a bit red.

"You look — *different*, close to."

Diane laughs nervously. "Different — better, or different — worse?" she asks.

"Just different — different," he says, and his voice is soft. He hasn't let go of her arm, but neither of them seems to notice or find it strange.

"And you — you're not how you look," she says, and, funnily enough, they each know exactly what the other one means.

"Would you like to dance?" Chris says.

SCENE 7

— The girls' side .

"Excuse me, but I noticed you sitting all by yourself . . ."

"Honestly!" Fiona says crossly. "My friend went to use the phone and never came back. I don't know whether to risk losing this table and go and look for her or what."

"How about if we had a dance and then you could look round for her at the same time?" Adam says.

"That'd be nice!" Fiona says, smiling suddenly.

They dance.

"Hey — is that her?" Adam asks.

"Yes! With your friend, isn't it?"

"That's right!"

"And just *look* at them," Fiona says wonderingly, and there's the tiniest bit of envy in her voice. "They're in a world of their own . . ."

"And *he* said he didn't fancy her!" Adam says in astonishment.

"That's what *she* said!"

They look at each other and laugh — and it's then that Something Else happens.

"Oh well," he says, "we won't interrupt." He changes, mid-dance, and starts moving slowly. His arm goes around Fiona but she doesn't object. In fact, she quite likes it.

Stage front. A small person wearing gold wings and a white loin-cloth affair hurries off. He looks rather smug, as well he might . . .

Continued from page 81

So they got to work . . .

HELLO. MY NAME IS ZAK. I WAS TOLD TO REPORT HERE TO HELP SOMEONE—

WHAT? THERE MUST BE SOME MISTAKE. MALE AND FEMALE AREN'T ALLOWED TO WORK TOGETHER. OR EVEN STUDY TOGETHER!

HMMM. I'D BETTER REPORT TO AN OFFICIAL THEN, AND—

OH—MUST WE? YOU KNOW, IT MIGHT BE A BIT OF FUN, WORKING TOGETHER.

RIGHT, WE'LL STACK THE VIDEO TAPES ON THE LEFT, AND THE MICRO- DISCS ON THE RIGHT, TO BEGIN WITH.

OK.

And they started talking . . .

But there was nothing to stop them now . . .

I'VE SEEN YOU AROUND SCHOOL. YOUR CLASS IS USUALLY LEAVING A ROOM AS WE COME IN. WE'VE NEVER HAD A CHANCE TO TALK.

WELL, WE'VE NEVER HAD PERMISSION, EITHER!

SO YOU'VE BEEN IN YOUTH CITY A YEAR NOW, ASTRA? HOW DO YOU LIKE IT?

WELL, IT'S OK. BUT WE DON'T HAVE MUCH CHOICE, DO WE? WE HAVE TO LIKE IT.

Then . . .

ZAK—COME AND HAVE A LOOK AT THIS. WHAT IS IT?

I DON'T KNOW. I'VE NEVER SEEN ANYTHING LIKE IT BEFORE . . .

HEY, THERE ARE A COUPLE MORE DOWN HERE!

Zak and Astra were puzzled, but as they opened the protective cover . . .

OH, I REMEMBER—IT'S A MAGAZINE! THIS IS HOW THEY LOOKED BEFORE EVERYTHING WAS PUT ON TO VIDEO TAPE. WE WERE SHOWN ONE IN HISTORY RECENTLY.

YES—I REMEMBER NOW, TOO. BUT LOOK HOW OLD THEY ARE. THE DATE SAYS 1981 . . .

HOW STRANGE AND OLD-FASHIONED EVERYTHING LOOKS.

I WISH WE HAD TIME TO READ THEM ALL RIGHT NOW. IT'S IMPOSSIBLE, THOUGH.

BUT WE'LL BE WORKING HERE FOR A WEEK OR TWO. WE COULD TAKE A LITTLE TIME OFF EVERY DAY, TO READ THROUGH THEM.

YES—I DON'T SEE WHY NOT.

And that's what they did . . .

THEY REFER TO SOMETHING CALLED ROMANCE AN AWFUL LOT, DON'T THEY? WHAT IS IT, I WONDER?

I DON'T KNOW—BUT EVERYONE DID SEEM TO BE OBSESSED BY IT.

IT SEEMS THAT MALE AND FEMALE WERE ALLOWED TO MIX QUITE FREELY IN THOSE DAYS . . .

AND CHILDREN LIVED WITH THEIR PARENTS INSTEAD OF BEING SEPARATED. HOW ODD!

The less they understood . . .

AND—AND WHAT IS THIS THING CALLED—LOVE?

I DON'T KNOW. BUT I REMEMBER, WHEN I WAS YOUNGER AND LIVING IN NURSERY CITY, THE MAYOR GAVE A SPEECH ABOUT LOVE . . .

AND DO NOT CONCERN YOURSELVES WITH LOVE. IT IS OLD-FASHIONED AND OBSOLETE AND STANDS IN THE WAY OF PROGRESS!

BUT I DON'T KNOW ABOUT THAT ANY MORE. LOVE SOUNDS AND LOOKS QUITE NICE TO ME.

But one thing Astra and Zak did understand was the need for caution . . .

IF THE OFFICIALS EVER FOUND OUT ABOUT THIS, WE'D BE PUNISHED. AND THEY WOULD CERTAINLY DESTROY THE MAGAZINES!

I KNOW . . .

So in stolen hours, in secret, they learned about a Patches-kind-of-world . . .

AND ONE THING ALWAYS PUZZLES ME—THIS KISSING THAT EVERYONE SEEMS TO DO . . .

I—I THOUGHT WE MIGHT TRY IT? WOULD YOU LIKE TO?

ALL RIGHT—BUT IT SEEMS A RATHER STRANGE, FUMBLING, TICKLISH PASTIME . . .

But also rather nice . . .

Continued on page 88

BAD MANNERS ARE CATCHING

... so we thought we'd meet some before they set out to capture the country!

Tracy Simons and Melissa Sanders, two fourteen-year-olds from West London, had the time of their lives when they went to see Bad Manners in the recording studio!

Melissa (in the yellow mac) and Tracy at the recording studios. "The whole group started joking around as soon as we arrived," said Melissa with a smile. "There wasn't time to be nervous, we were too busy having a good time!"

Sidesplitters

Barber: Well, sir, how would you like your hair cut?
Customer: Off!

Q: What did the beaver say to the tree?
A: It's been nice gnawing you.

My boyfriend has a good head for money — it's got a little slot in the top.

At the scene of a breakdown.
Driver: Hey, are you a mechanic?
Passerby: No, I'm a McDonald.

For goodness' sake! I must have told you a *million* times *not* to exaggerate!

Did you hear about the young ghost who got very scared when his friends told him too many human stories?

Nurse: Can I take your pulse now, sir?
Patient: Why — haven't you got one of your own?

Customer: Waiter, this plate's damp!
Waiter: Yes, I know sir, that's the soup.

Q: Do you write with your left hand or your right hand?
A: Neither, I write with a ballpoint pen!

Q: Are you going to take a bath?
A: No, I'm going to leave it where it is.

Lady: I never know what to do with my hands while I'm talking.
Young Man: Why not try holding them over your mouth?

Doctor: Take 3 teaspoonfuls of this medicine after each meal.
Patient: But I've only got two teaspoons.

Judge: Have you ever been up before me before?
Prisoner: I don't know, your honour. What time do you usually get up?

Customer: I want a nice piece of bacon. And make it lean.
Butcher: Which way, madam?

1st Man: I had to give up tap-dancing.
2nd Man: Oh, why?
1st Man: I kept falling in the sink.

Bad Manners acquire some new brass players . . . er . . . the guys aren't sure if the girls will pass their audition!

"Bad Manners always look as though they're having a good time when you see them on TV," said Tracy, "and it's nice to see that they're just as crazy in real life!"

Looks like Bad Manners hit the right note with our Special Reporters!

Doug Trendle checks out his new backing singers! "They gave us a guided tour of the studio which was a real laugh," said Tracy. "I thought they were really nice."

"I thought they were great, too," said Melissa. "Success couldn't have happened to a nicer group!"

1st Man: Excuse me, can you tell me the time?
2nd Man: I'm sorry, but I'm a stranger here myself.

Child: Mummy, there's a man at the door with a bill.
Mother: Don't be silly dear. It must be a duck with a hat on.

A man bought a bath and was just leaving the shop with it when the shop assistant called, "Do you want a plug?" "Why?" asked the man. "Is it electric?"

Angry employer: You should have been here at nine o'clock.
Late employee: Why, what happened?

1st Man: I washed my dog last night and he died.
2nd Man: Died? But why? Washing a dog can't kill it.
1st Man: Well, it was either that or the spin dryer that did it!

Q: Did you know that deep breathing kills germs?
A: Yes, but how do you get them to breathe deeply?

Q: What is furry, crunchy and makes a noise when you pour milk on it?
A: Mice crispies.

Customer: Waiter! There's a fly in my soup.
Waiter: Would you prefer it served separately, sir?

Customer: Have you got asparagus?
Waiter: No, we don't serve sparrows, and my name is *not* Gus!

Man: My dog plays chess with me.
Friend: That's amazing! It must be a really intelligent animal!
Man: Not really. I've won three games to two so far this evening.

POPWORD ANSWERS

1 Snowploughs, 2 Snowman, 3 Pantomimes, 4 Ronnie Corbett, 5 Larry Hagman, 6 Annie Lennox, 7 Jimmy Savile, 8 Eddie Kidd, 9 Gladys Knight, 10 Miss Piggy, 11 Rockford Files, 12 Kenny Everett, 13 Gambaccini, 14 Christmas Eve, 15 Funfairs, 16 Elvis Costello, 17 Cliff Richard, 18 Penelope Keith, 19 Rudolph, 20 Terry Wogan, 21 Presents, 22 Robin Cousins, 23 The Shadows, 24 Fawlty Towers, 25 Snowballs, 26 Angela Rippon, 27 Debbie Harry, 28 Happy New Year, 29 Isla St Clair.

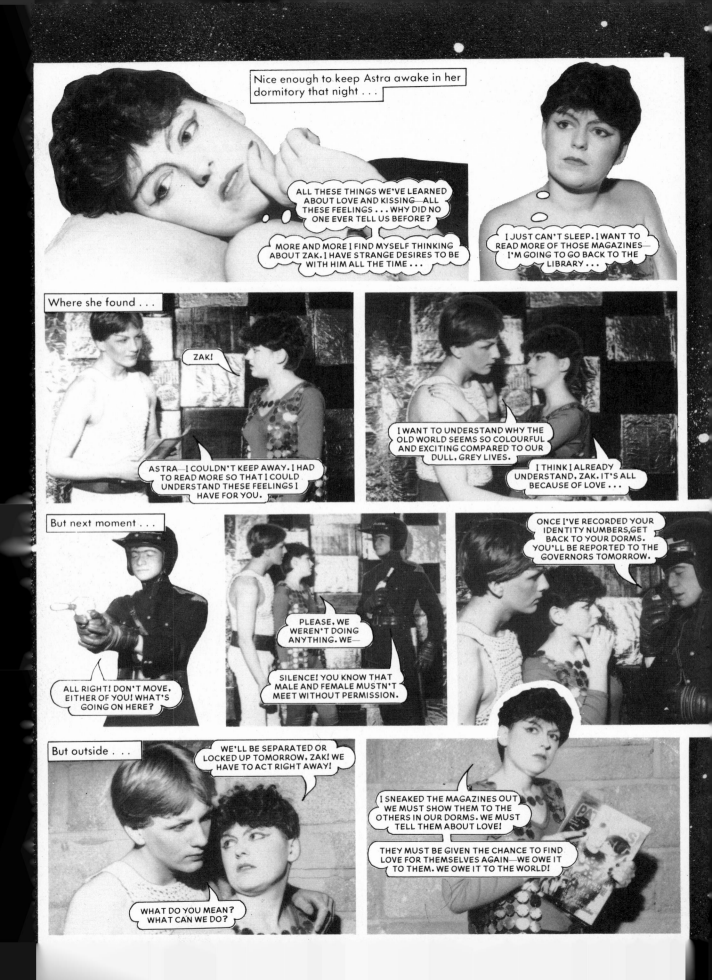

I DON'T KNOW. FROM THE LOOK OF SOME OF THE STORIES, LOVE CAN HURT—IT CAN BE VERY SAD.

BUT IT FEELS SO WONDERFUL, TOO. ISN'T SUCH HAPPINESS WORTH A LITTLE RISK, ZAK?

OF COURSE IT IS! YOU'RE RIGHT!

So . . .

. . . AND THE OFFICIALS HAVE BANNED LOVE AND TAKEN IT OUT OF SOCIETY!

THIS—PATCHES-KIND-OF-WORLD DOES SOUND MUCH MORE FREE AND HAPPY.

YOU MEAN WE WOULDN'T BE KEPT AWAY FROM OUR RELATIVES, IN YOUTH CITY AND CHILD CITY AND NURSERY-CITY?

THEY AREN'T CITIES, VIDA! THEY'RE PRISONS!

AND NOW WE WANT OUT!

By the time the police came for Astra and Zak it was much too late! The demonstrations and marches had begun . . .

People demanded the right to know about love again, and to learn about romance and marriage . . .

They became known in later history as the love protests!

The government was overthrown, and eventually love returned to a world where it had been lost . . .

AND ALL BECAUSE THE OFFICIALS DIDN'T COUNT ON THE DESIRE OF PEOPLE EVERYWHERE TO LOVE AND BE LOVED.

THEY DIDN'T COUNT ON OUR NATURAL INSTINCTS FOR LOVE AND AFFECTION.

But most of all . . . they just didn't count on Patches still being around!

WINTER'S WARMER WITH MADNESS!

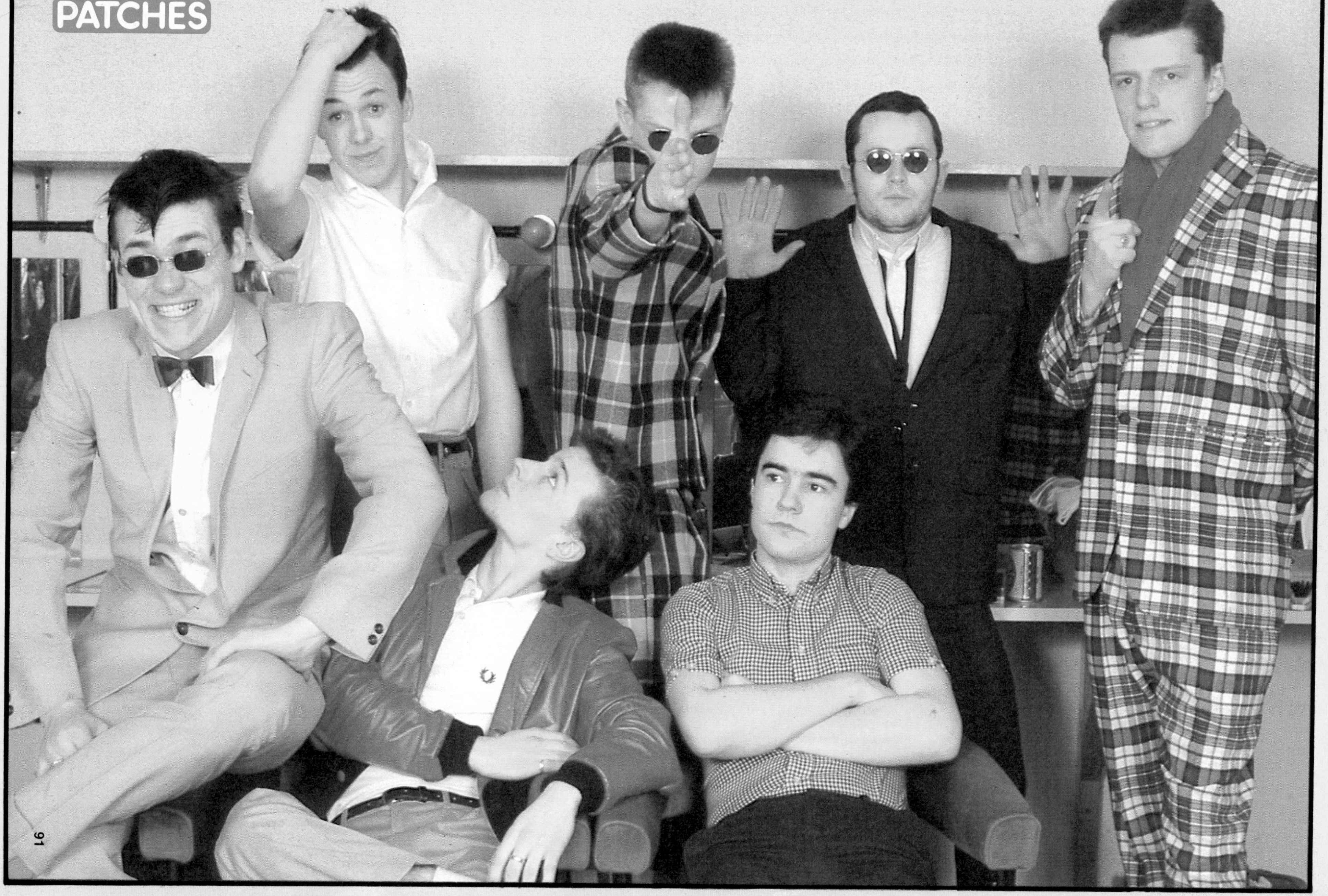

My parents were pretty fussy about who I went out with, but I knew they'd really like John. As long as they didn't find out about his sister . . .

I WAS SCARED

SHE wasn't one of my friends, and there wasn't any possibility that she ever would be, so when John said, that first night when he walked me home from the disco, "Hey, my sister's probably in your class. Kelly, her name is . . ." I just said, "Oh, yeah. She is in my class."

I tried not to let him see how disappointed I was. Up until that moment I'd been making a few plans in my head, about the next time I saw John properly, on a real date. But now I'd have to think again. If he was Kelly Fraser's brother, I wasn't sure that I ought to see him again.

But when he rang me during the week, and invited me to go to the pictures with him, I found myself saying yes. I'd been thinking about him, far too much for my own safety, thinking about the way I'd felt when I was with him, the buzz of excitement that I'd felt right down to my fingertips when he'd smiled across the room at me. I *had* to see him again.

And then Kelly sauntered up to me the next day at break with that confident sneer on her face and said, "I hear my brother's got lumbered with you, Linda Field? Well, don't let me hear you've been talking about me to him, that's all. I'll see to it that you don't go out with him for long if you do. I could do a bit of talking myself, and who's going to prove whether I'm telling the truth or not?" And then she sniggered, and walked off to join Tracy and Jan.

She hadn't been at our school for very long, only about three months or so. They'd all moved down from Scotland, someone said. I hadn't liked her from the first moment I saw her. There was something really shifty about her. She had those strange eyes that never looked straight at you, but always seemed to be examining your shoes, and she had a tight, hard mouth that never smiled, except in a sort of twisted leer.

And she made it clear that most of us weren't worth bothering about. She finally palled up with Tracy and Jan, the two really tough girls in the class that we'd always avoided. Together, the three of them giggled and sniggered through lessons, skived off school, and never did any homework.

I AVOIDED HER

I'd always left her alone. Mum and Dad are pretty strict about my friends, and I could just imagine what they'd say if I made friends with *her*, and acted the way she did, in or out of class. They'd even stopped me going round to Rose's house after Dad had seen her smoking in the street one day. Kelly Fraser would have given him a heart attack!

But the funny thing was, John was completely different. He was tidy and well spoken, not at all like his scruffy sister who exaggerated her Scottish accent so much that hardly anyone could understand her. And he wasn't loud and agressive, the way she was. He told me he was in his first year at the Technical College, studying accountancy.

I found it hard to see any similarities between him and the girl who tried to nick someone's maths exercise book to copy the homework answers from . . .

All through the second date, I was weighing him up, wondering how he could be so different from Kelly, or whether it was just an act. It didn't *seem* to be an act, though. He was waiting for me exactly where he said he would, at exactly the right time, looking really smart, and with the wonky little smile on his face that had burned me up the week before.

My staring at him made him nervous. He kept asking me if there was anything wrong, but really I couldn't find anything wrong with him at all. He was

Somehow I'd expected him to tighten up in our house. I'd thought he'd be worried about meeting Mum and Dad. But he wasn't. *I* was the one who made him nervous. With Mum and Dad he was easy, relaxed, really at home, and so courteous that he deserved several medals.

I could tell by Mum's smile, and the best coffee cups, that she was as impressed as I was by John's quiet good humour and his easy manners. Dad was looking pretty pleased, too, which was a miracle for him. According to him, no-one was good enough for me.

Mum kept offering John more cake, until he had to refuse the third slice.

"No thanks! I couldn't eat any more!" he told her. "But it was great. There's only one other person I know who can bake as well as that!"

"Your mother?" Mum smiled.

But John had noticed. When I glanced at him he was looking down at his hands, his shoulders slumped.

"Tell me about this new girl in your class, Linda," he said, quietly. "It *is* Kelly, isn't it?"

I TOLD HIM EVERYTHING

I burst out crying, then. I don't know what made me do that — perhaps the tension that had been building up in me, slowly, all evening, perhaps the fear that Kelly would carry out her threat, perhaps the shock of discovering that there were two Kellys, and one of them had managed to cope with her mother's death, and looking after a large family.

"Please, Linda," John begged. "Please tell me, for Kelly's sake."

mind, wasn't it? I suppose I suspected that Kelly would have to break down somehow, somewhere. So it's at school, is it? She's always been very clever, very interested in school . . ."

He shook his head as if it was all very difficult to understand. But he looked as if he was trying very hard.

"She was closest to Mum," he went on carefully. "I knew it all hit her hard. But she had to keep going at home, you see. We've expected too much from her really. She's not even had a chance to breathe, let alone cry. I'll talk to Dad. There has to be something we can do. And don't you worry. You did the right thing telling me about it!"

"Did I?" I sniffed.

"Sure you did. And tell you what, there's something else you can do," he whispered, just brushing the end of my nose

OF HIS SISTER

funny, and quiet, and so well-mannered that I knew Mum and Dad just couldn't object. Not unless they met his sister. And they weren't going to meet her, only him.

It's one of the rules Mum and Dad have, that any boy who takes me out comes in for a cup of coffee when he brings me home. It's quite a sensible rule, most of the time, and I don't mind about it. This time I was worried, though. I just prayed that Mum wouldn't ask too many questions, and realise that the awful new girl in our class that I'd sounded off about more than once was John's sister.

THEY LIKED HIM

What with one thing and another — my staring, the trembly way John made me feel, my worry about him saying the wrong thing to Mum and Dad, and his nervousness about what was wrong with me — the date didn't go as well as I'd hoped. We were both too strung up.

And by the time we arrived back at our house, I think both of us were in a state of panic. I couldn't even tell John what I was panicking about. If I told him what his sister was like and why I was worried about what *he* was really like, Kelly's threat would go into action. I had no doubt about that at all. And I wanted to see John again. I really did.

"No," John said quietly. "Mum died. That's why we moved down here, to be a bit closer to Dad's family. It's not my mother who bakes like that, it's my sister. She's a fantastic cook!"

No-one noticed my gasp. Mum was encouraging John to talk, and he was enthusiastic enough to need very little encouragement. But I couldn't believe what he was saying.

"Your sister looks after you, then?" Mum asked.

"Yes!" John said. "Five of us, including Dad! She's one in a million, my sister. You ought to see her with the little ones, just the image of Mum, she is, telling them off, then cuddling them better. She keeps the house spotless, shops, cooks, takes the kids to school, and meets them to bring them home. Dad says he'd be lost without Kelly!"

"Kelly?" Mum raised her eyebrows. "Kelly Fraser . . . I've heard that name. Isn't that the name of that dreadful new girl in your class, Linda? The one who's always trying to copy homework, and cheeks the teachers? Weren't you telling me . . . ?"

"Oh, no! That's someone else!" I gulped, pleased to notice that she'd lost interest and was persuading Dad to help her clear the coffee cups away, and help her with the washing-up. She didn't notice the gulp, or the mixture of embarrassment and bewilderment on my face. She just smiled, and shooed Dad out of the room.

He took my hand in his, and that made it easier to tell him about the other Kelly, the one who skipped school and messed about in lessons, the one everyone hated. And I told him about her threats, too.

He didn't say anything while I was talking and sobbing. He just sighed. And then, when I'd finished, he wiped my tears away with his hand, and tried to smile.

"I knew there was something wrong with you tonight," he said. "It was all this on your

with his lips. "When we've talked to Kelly, and found her some help in the house, and given her a chance to be an ordinary girl, she'll be needing a friend, a real friend. Fancy the job? My girl, and Kelly's friend?"

I wasn't very sure about that. Kelly Fraser still terrified me. But I'd heard her brother telling me what she was really like, and I believed him. He had the sort of face I could trust. And he gave me confidence, too — especially when he called me his girl . . .

Continued from page 3

DAVID, YOU'VE STILL GOT YOUR OLD JEANS ON!

SORRY, JENNY, I WAS DOING SOME WORK AND I DIDN'T HAVE TIME TO CHANGE.

Once we got inside I relaxed . . .

I DON'T CARE ABOUT THE REST OF THEM WHEN I'M WITH JENNY. EVEN IF I GAVE UP DANCING—I COULDN'T GIVE HER UP.

WOULD YOU STILL SEE ME IF I DIDN'T DANCE, JENNY?

DON'T BE SILLY, DAVID, YOU DO DANCE—AND BRILLIANTLY!

OH WELL, LOOKS LIKE I'LL HAVE TO KEEP ON DANCING! THE GUYS ARE BOUND TO FIND OUT SOONER OR LATER, BUT WHO CARES?

SEE YOU ON SATURDAY FOR THE FINALS THEN!

YOU BET! WILD HORSES WOULDN'T KEEP ME AWAY!

LEATHER-JACKETED MATES WON'T EITHER!

So, on Saturday . . .

OH NO! THAT'S THE BUS GOING EARLY—WE'LL BE LATE!

WHAT ARE WE GOING TO DO?

CAN YOU SEND A TAXI TO THE BUS STOP AT GREEN STREET, PLEASE?

YES, SIR! ONE WILL BE FREE IN ABOUT HALF AN HOUR.

OH NO!

SORRY JENNY— HALF AN HOUR!

BUT IF WE'RE LATE WE'LL BE DISQUALIFIED!